T0377335

Structure and Changes of China's Financial System

By virtue of several theoretical models and hypotheses, this book is one of the earliest studies which systematically investigates the structure and changes of China's financial institutions.

To begin with, it examines the relation between state utility function and China's economic growth and reveals the formation and transition of China's state-owned financial institutional arrangements. Based on this analysis, the author studies the influence of monetization on the arrangements and the financial support to China's gradual reform, which have long been neglected by researchers. Also, the model of money demand that can explain the specific conditions of the gradual reform is built, as the neoclassical framework has been incapable of explaining China's financial performance. In the last chapter, it discusses the dilemma of property rights under the state-owned financial system, with the establishment of the credit equilibrium model and the dual model of bad debts.

With insightful theoretical analysis and empirical researches, this book will appeal to scholars and students in finance, economics and economic history.

Jie Zhang is a Professor and the Head of the International Monetary Institute, Renmin University of China. His main research interests lie in the financial institution and financial development in China.

China Perspectives

The *China Perspectives* series focuses on translating and publishing works by leading Chinese scholars, writing about both global topics and China-related themes. It covers Humanities & Social Sciences, Education, Media, and Psychology, as well as many interdisciplinary themes.

This is the first time any of these books have been published in English for international readers. The series aims to put forward a Chinese perspective, give insights into cutting-edge academic thinking in China, and inspire researchers globally.

Titles in economics currently include:

Internationalization of the RMB
Establishment and Development of RMB Offshore Markets
International Monetary Institute of the RUC

Chinese Macroeconomic Operation
Liu Shucheng

The Chinese Path to Economic Dual Transformation
Li Yining

Hyperinflation
A World History
Liping He

Game Theory and Society
Weiying Zhang

Structure and Changes of China's Financial System
Jie Zhang

China's Fiscal Policy
Theoretical and Situation Analysis
Gao Peiyong

For more information, please visit www.routledge.com/series/CPH

Structure and Changes of China's Financial System

Jie Zhang

Routledge
Taylor & Francis Group

LONDON AND NEW YORK

First published in English 2018
by Routledge
2 Park Square, Milton Park, Abingdon, Oxon OX14 4RN

and by Routledge
711 Third Avenue, New York, NY 10017

Routledge is an imprint of the Taylor & Francis Group, an informa business

Published in Chinese by China Renmin University Press, 2011

British Library Cataloguing-in-Publication Data
A catalogue record for this book is available from the British Library

Library of Congress Cataloging-in-Publication Data
A catalog record for this book has been requested

ISBN: 978-1-138-90014-1 (hbk)
ISBN: 978-1-315-70746-4 (ebk)

Typeset in Times New Roman
by Apex CoVantage, LLC

Contents

Figures

Tables

Introduction

1   State, property rights and institutional structure

The institutional structure of China is unique compared to other countries, and it can be summarized as the developed superstructure of strong control power, the decentralized understructure of great mobility but no rigorous and effective middle structure that coordinates between the superstructure and understructure. This is called the institutional "dual structure".

A very attractive evolution process is seen in the generation of this dual structure, where the sequence of action and the connection form of the two major factors, the state and property rights, function as the key to understanding the process. Theoretically, "The state theory and the property right theory constitute the two major foundations for understanding of the institutional structure"; "Since the state defines the property right, the state theory plays the fundamental role and the state bears the ultimate responsibility for the efficiency of the property right structure that results in economic growth, stagnation or recession"; and the effective analysis on the state can hardly be reached without the property rights (North, 1981, pages 17 and 21). This book makes an explanation that involves the process of generation and the dissolution of the feudal system. Feudalism is the key stage to define how the form of the property rights was generated in an institutional structure and connected to the state. According to our preliminary study, the state had its status established prior to feudalism in China, since it was directly engaged in the "creation" of feudalism. Since feudal lords acted as the direct agents of the feudal state, their relations with civilians were practically a relationship of control and supervision from top to bottom instead of an interdependent contractual relationship. When a feudal state was strong enough, the feudal lords playing the role as first-level agents did not enjoy the ownership but only controlled civilians and their properties on behalf of the state; in case of decline of the strength of a feudal state, feudal lords generally established their own organizations and directly exercised their control and ownership over civilians and their properties, in other words, they became the new feudal state. Therefore, the state has always dominated the form of property rights in China, while the weak contractual and property right protection relationship between civilians and feudal lords failed to produce a stable form of property rights and the corresponding capability of independent negotiation throughout the evolution of feudalism. In this way, the strength of the state and civilians in the form of property rights had been exposed to extreme imbalance after the dissolution of feudalism, the powerful control by the state versus the decentralized and weak form of property rights. It has decided the basic trend and performance of the evolution of Chinese economic history.

In comparison, feudalism in Western Europe presented another picture, mostly distinctively characterized by establishment of the contractual relationship between feudal lords and civilians before the emergence of states. Once this kind of contractual relationship was confirmed, feudal lords gradually became the intermediate buffering role between the monarch and civilians and tended to protect civilians' interests in case of external invasion. More importantly, lords were not agents of the monarch's interests in the strict sense. They owned a relatively independent form of property rights and often burst into various forms of competition (political or economic) with the monarch; where this competition existed, feudal lords did not treat civilians as they willed but were internally motivated to abide by the contract (North, 1981, page 129). Consequently, civilians had their own stable forms of property rights as well as the negotiation ability that protected their property rights in the long-lasting feudal system in Western Europe, which is the key to understanding the evolution of the institutional structure of Western Europe. Moreover, certain cost was demanded to protect the forms of property rights of civilians, so the lords had come to be aware that they demanded an organization featuring scale-economy advantages in protection of property rights (such as state) to protect property rights on behalf of themselves. The demand became even more urgent when the scale of trade and exchange went beyond the geographic restriction of these lords. In this way, the state was "naturally born" due to the demands for more economical protection of property rights from bottom to top by lords and civilians. The natural transmission of the protection of property rights from feudal lords to the state made the most attractive story in the whole process. Since the state was established based on people's internal demands, and the form of property rights had accumulated adequate negotiation ability upon the emergence of the state, the state was able to develop contractual relationships with various forms of property rights and maximize the rent for protection of property rights, and it was impossible to exert unilateral control. As a result, the state protects property rights by supplying institutional products without direct interference or control over the economic process, while businessmen, enterprises and other economic organizations voluntarily pay certain fees (tax) to purchase institutional products and accept the protection of property rights by the state. Under these circumstances, enterprises, banks and many efficient economic organizations have rapidly risen and become the major contributors to economic growth. Meanwhile, the institutional middle structures including property right structure, market structure and law structure, and so forth, have been confirmed and gradually improved, giving birth to the ultimate institutional triple structure.

It is important to note that the economic freedom and form of property rights acquired by the understructure after the dissolution of feudalism in China failed to reach consistency with the protection of property rights by the state. In this case, the economic freedom and form of property rights of the understructure are extremely unstable, while the state provides only the control from top to bottom instead of the equal protection of property rights. Therefore, the isolated form of property rights of the understructure has no stable economic expectation. Even with certain capital accumulation and investment capability, there is not enough motivation for investment on economic growth. Under the dual structure, the form of property rights without protection shows no close link to economic growth, while the state bears the sole responsibility for capital accumulation and investment and economic growth, and its capability and preference determine the performance of economic growth and the efficiency of resource allocation. Without doubt, as the state holds the largest share of resources under the dual structure, economic growth only depends on promotion by the state. The high-positive correlation between investment by the state and economic growth makes up one basic characteristic of the evolution of the dual structure.

In this respect, the Forging Ahead Strategy implemented since the 1950s was a necessary consequence of the evolution of the dual structure. Superficially, the state, the one who decides the economic strategies, had no other choice but to resort to this strategy and a series of supporting institutional arrangements. It can be imagined, in a triple structure, that the economic and efficiency of resource allocation could not be unilaterally decided by either party but should be the result of integrating preferences of both the state and single forms of property rights under the specific property right structure and market structure. Either the state or the single form of property rights starts from an initial endowment point, exchanges for their preferences in the market and reaches the equilibrium point after transaction, where the preferences of all parties are considered. Economic policies and resource allocations emerging on this basis would definitely strike a balance of the maximum interests of all parties and thus would be the closest to Pareto efficiency. However, in a dual structure, preference is only given to the state but not to other forms of property rights, while no equilibrium point is generated in the economy of single preference. In other words, no other preference pulls the state preference from the initial point to the equilibrium point. The allocation of resources failing to reach the equilibrium point apparently makes it impossible to realize Pareto efficiency. The outcome of implementation of the Forging Ahead Strategy proves this point sufficiently.

The economic reform initiated since the late 1970s has boosted economic growth rapidly, fundamentally because the economic freedom of the understructure that had been constrained by the centrally planned economic system was released, bringing about great motivation and incentive to economic growth. Nevertheless, the growth potential and reform incentive merely relying on the economic freedom of the understructure is far from enough for long-term economic growth, and support by the middle structure is demanded. Specifically, only when the middle structure is established can the growth potential and incentive of the understructure be rationally mobilized and allocated and thus transformed to economic growth. For example, the reform of state-owned enterprises in China has been relatively successful in solving the incentive mechanism but unsuccessful in solving the issue of the system of manager selection (Zhang Weiying, 1995). The reason lies in that the former is an issue about the understructure, but the latter is about the middle structure or market selection. However active the understructure is, it has no connection with long-term economic growth without a stable and effective middle structure. The economic freedom of the understructure only renders the necessary condition for the establishment of an effective institutional structure, while the middle structure constitutes the sufficient condition, where people could fully exercise their economic freedom based on rules provided by the middle structure and the state could protect and adjust people's economic freedom through the middle structure. According to the observation over previous economic reforms from the original decentralization reform to the market-oriented reform afterwards, no significant achievement was made on establishing the middle structure, and the whole economic operation and resource allocation still largely rely on arrangements and control by the state (superstructure). The economy subject to these reforms is still placed in a dual structure, consisting of the powerful state and the understructure with increasing economic freedom. That is to say, the previous reforms failed to change the original logic of connection between the state and property rights; the state still dominates the forms of property rights, and economic growth is still driven by the state to a great extent. There are still unsettled issues of economic reforms in that how the state changes from direct control over the understructure to indirect control over the understructure relying on the middle structure establishes the contractual relation and protection of property rights between the state and the understructure and makes economic growth the result of integrating the state and property rights.

2   The financial system in the dual structure

Theoretically, the financial system is a kind of institutional arrangement that saves the transaction costs and improves efficiency of resource allocation; it is not arbitrarily generated or changed or artificially arranged according to certain wills or external modes, and it is not only a tangible framework but also a result of a series of interdependent evolution processes. In a triple structure, the financial institutions, being the basic factor to the financial system, come into being based on a logical social division of labor, while the social division of labor develops based on the expansion of the market scope. Specialized producers only emerge and exist when social demand on certain product or service reaches a certain level along with the expansion of the market, which is the highlight of the so-called Smith Theorem. In terms of the evolution of the industrial structure, first, a farmer produced the surplus that he/she could not independently consume and proposed the demand on exchange for the surplus products of others; the currency arising along with the development of exchanges led to the revolution and specialization of exchanges; and the specialized exchanges vigorously expanded the room for resource allocation and scope of production and further promoted division of labor in exchanges, thus contributing to the generation of banks and financial institutions. Douglass C. North was also concerned about this logic process in his theoretical framework of institutional changes. According to him, institutions are gradually developing and changing along with market expansion, specialization and frequent capital flow. Take the financial system as an example. First, people made certain innovations to the transaction mode for the sake of promoting capital flow and saving transaction costs, such as the evolution of the bills of exchange and development of bills discounting. Later, along with expansion of transactions, people requested utilization and development of exchange centers, which were first the fair, then the bank and finally the financial institutions specialized for bills discounting. Therefore, the development of financial institutions is "not only the function of specific institutions, but also the function of the scale of economic activities" (North, 1990).

However, the arrangements of the financial system in the dual structure follow special logic, and its function greatly varied from that in the triple structure. As discussed prior, the state functions as the major pusher for savings mobilization, capital formation and economic growth, while the funds for economic growth are insufficient in most cases. Under the circumstances, the financial system was "created" by the state from top to bottom to solve the fund shortage. Furthermore, the financial system in the dual structure first follows the preference of the superstructure (state) instead of the demands of the understructure.

Due to these differences in logic, the financial system in the dual structure could be created or abolished, expanded or shrunk totally based on the preference of the state, and its function changes from saving transaction costs and improving the efficiency of resource allocation to collecting and controlling financial resources. It serves the mode of economic growth favored by the state and the goal of rent maximization to the utmost.

Since the financial system is created by the state, it is undoubtedly under direct control by the state. However, interestingly, the emergence of a financial system created by the state suggests that other financial systems not created by the state are informal. No matter how the informal financial systems satisfy the general logic for institutional evolution and the financial demands of the understructure, they will be finally integrated by the formal financial system. Informal financial systems often suffer disorder due to lack of the middle structure, and their financial behaviors often conflict with the goal of rent maximization of the state and fail to satisfy the financial demands of the understructure. However, whatever happens, it is the basic rule of the dual structure that the demands of the understructure should be inferior to the demands of the superstructure, and the financial system is no exception.

Take the practical evolution process of the Chinese financial system for example. As demonstrated by historical findings, some primitive financial (credit) institutional arrangements emerged when feudalism was established in China, such as Quan Fu (local authority governing tax, borrowing and interest, etc.) in Western Zhou Dynasty. Since then, various financial forms arose in the Northern and Southern Dynasties, Sui and Tang Dynasty, including Gui Fang (the private business safekeeping the wealth of others), Gong Xie Qian (fund allocated by the central government for government-run businesses), Fei Qian (bills for exchange for money), pawnshops opened by the government and private pawnshops and so forth; by modern times, new financial arrangements successively emerged, such as the sliver shop, the old-style Chinese bank, the old-style firm for the exchange of money, the official currency bureau and so on. In general, most of these financial arrangements were not produced by the financial demands of the understructure, while industry investment did not constitute the major goal of these financial resources. The Chinese financial arrangements directly established by the superstructure from the beginning were all created for fiscal needs, such as Gong Xie Qian in the Sui Dynasty, which borrowed money and acquired interests for government use, and those established by private individuals were mostly for commercial purposes. For example, Kato Shigeshi (1959, page 412) believed that the Gui Fang in the Tang Dynasty was born based on merchants' demands mainly for commercial purpose. As a matter of fact, a special distribution structure of benefiting opportunities exists in the whole society under the dual structure, where benefiting opportunities are mostly distributed in the superstructure of the society and the industries making profits in the short term but are rarely seen in other key industries to long-term economic growth due to no property right protection mechanism and no stable profit expected. The financial (credit) industry is the one making profits in the short term. Therefore, the accumulated private capitals undoubtedly fight for this industry. Also because of the aforementioned special distribution structure of benefiting opportunities, these newly established financial and credit institutes would not invest capitals on the industries that are valuable for long-term economic growth but show no short-term benefit, but rather would compete to be involved in commercial operation. As a result, the financial and credit institutional arrangements have been relatively active in cases of economic depression and relatively chaotic economic order during the institutional evolution of China (Zhang Jie, 1993, page 209), as economic depression and disorder create the best opportunities to acquire short-term commercial benefits. Nevertheless, the superstructure always plays the dominating role in the dual structure, so the non-governmental financial industry has to reach a compromise with the superstructure of "violence potential" first no matter how active it is. It is commonly seen in institutional evolution that the non-governmental financial organizations reach consensus with the superstructure to jointly earn profits, such as the old-style firm for exchange of money in Shanxi (Zhang Jie, 1993, page 228). This is the profound reason why many financial forms in Chinese history ultimately failed to develop to be modern financial institutional arrangements.

The financial institutional arrangements in China in modern times still follow the existing logic in evolution. The first few modern banks in China (the Imperial Bank of China, 1897; the Bank of Ministry of Revenue of Qing, 1905; the Bank of Communications, 1907; and so on) were all established by the superstructure from top to bottom; while some were directly established by the central government, some were jointly founded by the government and private capitals, and some were established by local governments for the purpose of fiscal convenience. So-called non-government commercial banks (such as the oldest, Zhejiang Industrial

Bank, established in 1909) mostly pursued short-term commercial benefits but avoided investment in industries. This trend has been further intensified since the establishment of the Republic of China. The Beiyang government and Kuomintang government had successively set up the huge financial organization system to support fiscal needs, local governments all opened banks and other forms of commercial banks still applied numerous financial resources to business speculation. According to statistics, the 14 largest commercial banks in China including Kincheng Bank, China & South Sea Bank and the YiehYien Commercial Bank invested the majority of funds in real estate, with the total investment amount sharply increased from 3.47 million Yuan in 1921 to 61.44 million Yuan in 1936 and the corresponding profit from over 30,000 Yuan to 1.69 million Yuan. Among the 50 million Yuan, the total assets in the treasury of the Union Bank of Shanghai, real estate accounted for 82.6%. According to investigations in Chongqing, 89% of the outstanding loans in 15 financial institutes were commercial loans by the end of 1939, compared to 96% in 26 financial institutes by 1940, 89% in 36 financial institutes by 1941 and 80% in 60 financial institutes by late March 1942 (Zhang Jie, page 233).

The dual structure in modern and contemporary financial systems is mainly characterized by financial monopoly by the superstructure. According to statistics, by June 1946, the number of government-operated banks reached 2,446 out of the total 3,489 banks in the Kuomintang-controlled area at that time, accounting for over two-thirds. By the end of December of the same year, the four banks, two boards and one treasury (Bank of China, Bank of Communications, Farmers Bank of China, Central Bank of China, Central Trust of China, Postal Remittances and Savings Bank and Central Cooperative Bank) had their deposits occupy 91.7% of total deposits and their loans take up as high as 93.3% of total loans. After the foundation of the People's Republic of China, financial control and financial monopoly by the state could not be avoided due to the existence of the dual structure. The proportion of loans provided by government-operated banks in total loans rose rapidly from 58.6% in 1950 to 92.8% in 1952 (Yi Gang, 1996a, page 90). By the end of 1956, the state actually controlled the whole financial industry, leaving no financial institutional arrangement in any form in the understructure. This situation has been exposed to gradual changes since the economic reform in the late 1970s, but the state still holds the control and monopoly over finance despite all these reforms. In 1978 when the reform was initiated, the deposits of state-owned banks accounted for 87.23% and the loans accounted for 97.62%, which were still high, respectively 72.32% and 77.57%, by 1996. Based on the gross assets, the market share of state-owned banks in 1996 was approximately 75% (People's Bank of China, 1997, page 38).

However, it is a remarkable fact that the financial control and financial monopoly by the state after 1949 could be divided into two stages with the year of 1979 as the division. Before 1979, the state controlled finance to implement the Forging Ahead Strategy of the national economy; after 1979, the state continued to control finance for the demands of the gradual reform. It is interesting that the financial control in the two different stages led to completely different performances, as the gradual reform in the latter stage has achieved success compared to the failure of the Forging Ahead Strategy in the first stage.

This book aims to discuss the logical connection between the successful gradual reform in China after 1979 and the evolution of the financial system, as well as the necessity of the financial control by the state in the gradual reform, and further observes from the perspective of the evolution of the financial system to discover the special path leading the dual structure to the triple structure. As it should be, the description and analysis of the institutional changes (including the evolution of the financial system) in the longer period before 1979 may be of greater significance compared to the short-term investigation by this book, since the analysis would be more accurate and reasonable based on investigations on the longer period of institutional changes. This is undoubtedly a field of investigation of great potential and attraction in the future.

3   Some fundamental hypotheses

As this book attempts to incorporate the issue of the structure and evolution of the financial system in China in the framework of mainstream economics for discussion, some basic theoretical hypotheses shall be given first of all.

I   *Hypothesis of the rational state*

One great contribution of the institutional change theory to economics lies in proposing and adhering to the hypothesis of the rational state. The state here meanwhile incorporates the factor of the central government. The hypothesis of the rational state refers to the concept that the state has its own preference and utility function and calculates costs and benefits at all times during institutional changes. To be specific, faced with changes to the financial system and the efficient form of financial property rights, the state only takes the initiative to impel changes based on the maximum rent. The institutional innovation mainly originates from the superstructure instead of the electorate due to the cause of the "free rider". Therefore, the benefit-cost structure of a state seems extremely important during institutional changes. Changes to the relative prices and relative materiality among financial factors would lead to changes in the attitude of the state towards changes to the financial system (to relax or strengthen financial control). When the changes to the relative prices among financial factors make the control cost of the state smaller than the control benefits, the evolution and innovation of the financial system would be delayed. In this case, the state would protect the form of financial property rights that is favorable to maximum rent but ignore its influence on efficiency.

Since the state-owned financial property right form under state control constitutes the background and starting point of the evolution of the Chinese financial system, it is of particular significance to investigate changes to the cost-benefit structure of financial control by the state. If we believe that the institutional changes would generate numerous factors that increase the cost of financial control by the state, the state concession in finance or shrinking state-owned financial property rights would be unavoidable. However, if a large number of new financial property right forms of greater efficiency appear, the relatively inefficient state-owned financial property right form would suffer exterior competitive pressure and threats to its existence. Then the state would have to choose exiting the competition or changing the structure of the financial property rights to lower the cost of social transactions and thus improve the efficiency of the allocation of financial resources. From this point of view, the speed of changes to the state-owned financial property right form depends on the growth and competitive pressure of other financial property right forms. As a result, the state makes every attempt to restrict other financial property right forms from the beginning; otherwise the opportunity cost of electors' financial selection would be changed due to the development of other financial property right forms. As long as the opportunity cost of electors (savers and investors) remains unchanged, the low-efficiency state-owned financial property right form could survive. Therefore, the expansion of other financial property right forms is an important path to change the state-owned property right structure. Apparently, this conclusion requires support by the hypothesis of the rational state; otherwise, we could not effectively describe the true story of changes to the Chinese financial system and structure in the recent two decades.

II Hypothesis of local behaviors

Local behaviors play a special part in institutional changes due to the dual structure in China. Based on previous experiences of reforms, local behaviors have functioned as the protection of the new financial property right forms. Although local protection of the new financial property right forms also aims for maximum benefits, it objectively stimulates innovation of financial property rights and changes the existing financial system and structure. The local utility function is inevitably inconsistent with the utility function of the state, while the mutual game between the state and the local authority resulting from the inconsistency of the utility function exactly provides opportunities for expansion of new financial property right forms. Since Reform and Opening-Up, new financial property right forms such as local commercial banks and cooperative banks have emerged and developed based on protection by the local government.

As a matter of fact, local government seems to enjoy certain functions as the middle structure during institutional changes in China. As we know, the middle structure of China was born deficient, and only local governments bear the capability to negotiate with the state. In other words, in the dual structure of long-term contrast between the powerful country (superstructure) and weak society (understructure) in China, the "intermediate" role of the local governments should not be underestimated. When the local government of independent interests becomes the middleman to communicate between the will of the superstructure on institutional supply and the demand of the understructure on institutional innovation, it is possible to break the barrier of institutional innovation set up by the superstructure and realize the consistency between the maximum rent of the superstructure and the protection of efficient property right structure (Yang Ruilong, 1998). During institutional changes in China, the local government has had this dual nature. On one hand, it is an integral part of the superstructure of violence potential; on the other hand, it is closely linked to the economic interests of the understructure of the region and enjoys the strong economic and social function. Since the local government has combined both functions of the superstructure and the understructure, it naturally becomes the intermediary between the superstructure and the understructure during institutional changes. As local strength is gradually consolidated based on decentralization reform, the violence potential of the superstructure would be subject to great limitations and restrictions; since local interests and the interests of the understructure of the region show increasing consistency due to institutional changes, local governments would attach greater importance to the property right structure and economic incentives of the understructure for the sake of maximum interests, which directly decide the economic growth and social welfare of the region. Consequently, private property rights and non-state-owned economies have grown rapidly under local protection, such as the re-establishment of rural reform and peasants' property rights, development of rural enterprises, rise of private enterprises and emergence of local and private finance (non-state-owned finance). It can be seen that experiences of reforms in China show evident differences to the path of Western Europe in the earlier stage due to the factor of local governments. For example, the mechanism for protection of new property rights in rural area of China realizes a great number of formal and informal transactions with the state through the alliance of household with village area and local government instead of checking the state through individuals and the civic public sphere. The relation between the state and the society after change renders the environment for protection and execution of the property right contract upon primary definition. On this basis, more complex property right contracting forms will emerge in large number (Zhou Qiren, 1994).

Nevertheless, local government shows certain limitations or requires conditions in protecting the property rights since it bears part of the violence potential, after all. Being a part of the superstructure, the local government has its cost-benefit structure distinguished from a pure property right form or economic institute. For example, the structure of the state-owned financial property rights blindly pursues expansion of the scale of the financial institutes and competes with other local governments in rent-seeking, disregarding the influence on efficiency and thus resulting in uneconomical spatial distribution of financial institutions and irrational allocation of financial resources. This situation is completely understandable from the perspective of the function of the local governments' interest, while the fundamental issue still lies in the structure of state-owned financial property rights instead of local behaviors. Therefore, the situation mentioned prior and the low efficiency of allocation of financial resources are considered the necessary costs for the evolution of the financial system in this book. It is foreseeable that the capability of the new form of property rights to negotiate with the local government is gradually improving along with institutional changes, which is undoubtedly favorable for independent development of the new form of property rights.

When the new form of property rights has developed to a certain degree, its interest conflict with the superstructure will gradually become inferior to the rapidly rising conflicts with the local government, and the new form of property rights that grew under protection by the local government will necessarily pursue the real independence of property rights. In this way, the local government needs to transform from the unilateral "protection of property rights" from top to bottom for the purpose of maximum rent to the protection of property rights in real sense, while the new form of property rights will purchase and "consume" the protection. If all local governments follow this way of transformation, they would find it costs too much to separately protect the property rights, and therefore the protection of property rights would be transferred gradually from the local government to the superstructure (state). Then, as mentioned prior, the state would no longer unilaterally control the new form of property rights, but would have to exchange better protection of property rights for increase of rent.

1 The institutional structure, the state and state-owned financial institutional arrangements

1 The institutional structure and the role of the state

As an important proposition of the institution change theory, institutional structure determines the set and room of institutional choices. According to our previous analysis, due to the existence of varieties of forms of property rights and the property right protection mechanism, the spontaneous process of the property right forms pursuing maximum interests in Western Europe naturally led to the Industrial Revolution and boosted economic growth, while the state only played a limited role in the process. Although the status of the state was raised afterwards, its role in economic growth has not been exposed to significant changes, as economic growth is still the result of competition, negotiation and compromise among several property right forms and interest groups (also undoubtedly incorporating factors such as technical progress) instead of depending on the preference of any party.

However, the dual institutional structure of China has created limited institutional choices. Whenever faced with pressure on economic growth, only a few institutional arrangements could be applied in addition to state-owned property rights. In this way, the state has to independently carry out the mission of allocating resources and promoting economic growth. It is not the voluntary choice but the only choice for the state to play the role as the facilitator of industrialization. In other words, it is the product of the dual institutional structure.

Therefore, the idea proposed by the academia that the Forging Ahead Strategy implemented in China in the 1950s was a voluntary choice of the state (Lin Yifu et al., 1994, page 46) needs further discussion. According to this idea, the state might or might not have chosen the Forging Ahead Strategy at that time; that is to say, the state might also have chosen the progressive comparative advantage strategy. However, first, the dual structure had determined the choice of the state that the state was destined to play the role to promote industrialization and economic growth; and, second, once the state had taken on the role, it was impossible to select the comparative advantage strategy, which did not conform to the behavior function and interest preference of the state and meanwhile was not the strength of the state. The edge of the state lies in its "violence potential", which goes beyond the preference of other property right forms and vigorously promotes industrialization.

Since the state functions as the facilitator of industrialization, the speed and pushing approaches of industrialization naturally follow the preference of the state and the utility function. As is known to us, under normal conditions, the efficiency of resource allocation and economic growth depend on the equilibrium point existing in the property right transaction, and Pareto optimality of resource allocation is achieved upon the equilibrium point of the property right transaction. Nevertheless, there is no equilibrium point in resource allocation in the single preference of the state, as the efficiency of resource allocation is solely decided by the economic decisions of the state. Due to no property right transaction or corresponding market structure, the efficient mechanism to search, process and display information could hardly be generated, leading to the high information cost that directly influences the accuracy of decisions; the correcting mechanism in the process of economic decision making and economic operation is also excluded as the property right competition is rejected. In the end, the efficiency of resource allocation largely relies on the unilateral judgement of the decision-makers, and errors in decision making and resource allocation are common in economic operation. This situation should not be simply attributed to the errors of decision making by the state; the fundamental cause should be the dual structure itself. When one preference was free from any external constraint by other preferences, no matter who owned the preference (local government or the enterprise), it would come to the same result.

2 The state model and its extended explanation

Since the state plays the role to boost industrialization and economic growth in China, it is necessary to come to understand the state model. As a kind of institutional arrangement in the state-led industrialization, state-owned financial institutions could be explained from the state model.

According to Douglass North (1981), the state model always occupies a prominent position in any analysis of long-term evolution. As the state functions as the key to economic growth as well as the source for artificial economic recession, the paradox makes the state the core of research in economic history (page 20). In China, the state model is of particular significance due to the special relationship between the state and industrialization, so the process of industrialization and institutional evolution in China could hardly be understood without understanding of the state model.

After giving a simple definition of the state and commenting on two relevant ideas (the contract theory and predatory theory), Douglass North proposed a simple state model, which consists of three hypotheses. First, the state exchanges incomes with services for the state enjoys the scale economy advantage in this respect (providing protection of property rights); second, the state always attempts to act as a monopolist with discrimination and designs the property rights based on maximum income of its own; and, third, the design of property rights and behavior selection by the state are subject to constraints by other property right forms (i.e., potential competitors), so "the degree of the monopoly power of the ruler is a function of the closeness of substitutes for the various groups of constituents" (North, 1981, page 22–24).

Some extended explanations may be given to adapt the state model of Douglass North to conditions in China. First, we notice that in China, the state is independent from the logic of property right protection and basically has no function to exchange incomes (tax incomes) with protection of property rights, so the growth of incomes shows no internal connection with the property right structure. The state gains incomes through approaches other than providing property right protection (and social justice), which determines the particularity in the ways to earn benefits by the state during industrialization in China. Second, theoretically, no other property right form exists, so the opportunity cost of voters goes to zero and the state is free from any internal potential property right competition; but the external potential competition always exists, while the competition would only strengthen the connection between the state and the industrialization process. Third, if the first and the third hypothesis are tenable, the behaviors of the "monopolist with discrimination" of the state would be subject to external constraints and could not unilaterally design or produce property rights according to North's state model. However, in view of these extended explanations, there is no constraint exerted by internal potential property right competition, and the state could absolutely design the property right structure that realizes and satisfies the utility function of its own based on the monopoly principle.

As also learned from the aforementioned state model, we could change the external conditions for the state to realize the maximum utility, although we could not alter the utility function of the state in a short period. It is a common thing that the state pursues the maximum rent according to our given rational hypothesis. Therefore, the efficiency of resource allocation depends on whether any other property right form that could compete with the state would restrict the state's pursuit for maximum utility, instead of whether the state exists or whether the state would realize the maximum utility and establish the corresponding institutional arrangement. Apparently, the key to institutional evolution lies in changing the environment and conditions for realizing the utility function but not attempting to change the utility function of the state. As long as no other property right form appeared, the opportunity cost of voters would not be exposed to any change, and the property right form of the state could survive no matter how low the efficiency is.

As a result, the difference between the state contract theory and predatory theory can be further explained as that once other property right forms could compete with the property right form of the state, the state would observe the competition principle instead of the monopoly principle, and then the state would compete with these property right forms, finally reach a compromise with them and form its own comparative advantage (i.e., bearing the obligation on property right protection). It means that the state does not take the initiative to pursue certain goal of social welfare, but only acts under the pressure of competition. However, once the state presents a monopoly, it would receive excessive "violence potential" through allocation, and would regulate on the property rights and allocate resources merely based on its own interests or preference.

3 State utility function, monopoly property rights and its expansion path

I State utility function: general descriptions

According to the state model and its extended explanations, the utility function of the state comprises two key variables.[1] The first is the pursuit for the monopoly property right form. Once the monopoly property right form was realized, the state would enjoy the right to control and dispose the social economic resources and social output surplus. The second is the pursuit for expansion of the "increment" of the monopoly property rights. After realizing monopoly and control over the existing "stock" of property rights, the state would become dissatisfied with the current scale of property rights. Since maximum rent and control over economic surplus constitute the increasing function for the scale of the monopoly property rights, the state would undoubtedly expand its increment of property rights after realizing the control over the stock of property rights.

It must be noted that in addition to these two key endogenous variables, the utility function of the state also involves some exogenous variables. Two of the exogenous variables draw the widest attention. The first is the property right structure, which decides whether any other property right form of adequate negotiation ability exists other than the state monopoly property right form. If it does exist, the utility pursuit of the state monopoly property rights would be exposed to restrictions. As mentioned prior, the dual institutional structure in China determines the pattern of "powerful country and weak society", laying a considerably favorable condition for the state to pursue the monopoly property right from and expand the increment of the property rights. The second is the external competition. According to Douglass North (1981),

> Stagnant states can survive as long as there is no change in the opportunity cost of the constituents at home or in the relative strength of competitor states. This last condition usually implies that the state approaches the status of a monopoly and is surrounded by weak states.
>
> (page 29)

The external competition generally promotes the state to pursue institutional innovation and improve efficiency. However, when the state pursues the monopoly property rights, the external competition only pushes the state to further strengthen the property right form.

II Monopoly property right form and nationalization

In view of the utility function of the state, the state prefers to pursue the monopoly property right form. Without any other property right form, the preference would rapidly drive the state to control the process of industrialization and economic growth. In this way, explanations to many problems could be found. Since

China had no other property right form of adequate negotiation ability in the 1950s, it had been very smooth for the state to pursue the monopoly property right form with its comparative advantage. For example, private plants of large scale had been gradually transformed to be joint public-private ownership since 1954, by which the state transformed the nature of property rights through penetrated investment; medium and small-sized enterprises had been exposed to change from independent enterprises to the joint public-private management of the whole sector and finally to the new state-owned property right form. In early 1956, nationalization of the whole sector had been completed, where the fixed-rate system of unified profit distribution was established to replace the previous independent profit distribution of each single enterprise, the previous enterprise owners lost their right in management and control and these property right forms were transformed to be state-owned property rights. Meanwhile, bureaucratic capitals (original monopoly property right form) were confiscated. Along with economic nationalization in 1956, monopoly over the property right forms by the state was realized. According to statistics, in the gross value of industrial output in 1952, state-owned enterprises took up 41.5%, compared to 3.3% of collective enterprises, 4% of joint state-private enterprises and 51.2% of private and individual enterprises; however, by 1956, the state-owned industrial output value occupied 67.5% of the gross value of industrial output, compared to 32.5% of joint state-private enterprises, when the original private industrial property right forms disappeared (Xue Muqiao, 1979, page 38). At the same time, the previous private property right form in agriculture had been rapidly transformed to be the monopoly property right form controlled and produced by the state through mutual aid and cooperation and the people's commune campaign (Zhou Qiren, 1994).

It is important to point out that according to our discussion, the transformation from private enterprises to state-owned enterprises and the people's commune campaign since the 1950s was not the industrialization strategy that gave priority to the development of heavy industry at the very beginning,[2] but was a result of the state seeking for the monopoly property right form based on its utility function. Even without pursuing the so-called rapid industrialization or the Forging Ahead Strategy, the state would still transform the property rights of private enterprises and integrate them to be state-owned property right forms under the background of the dual structure. Beyond any doubt, the formation of the monopoly property right form was objectively favorable for implementation of the Forging Ahead Strategy of the state. In other words, without establishment of the state-owned monopoly property right form, even though the state showed preference in pursuing rapid industrialization, the preference could not be translated to practices. Therefore, we believe that the dual structure has built the internal logic connection between the state and the Forging Ahead Strategy and that nationalization in China was the result of synthesis of the "endogenous variable" of the state pursuing the monopoly property right form based on the utility function and the "exogenous variable" of the dual institutional structure.

III Expansion of state-owned property right forms and the Forging Ahead Strategy

After completing nationalization of the stock of property rights, the state further sought for expansion of the state-owned monopoly property right form based on the utility function of the state. Several paths were available for expansion of the monopoly property rights at that time. The first was to expand the state-owned property rights and surplus control in agriculture. However, although agricultural production accounted for a large proportion of the gross national product (GNP) in China at that time, with agriculture averagely occupying 59.3% of national income from 1950 to 1953 and total value of agricultural output accounting for 70% of the total output in 1949, it only contributed very low surpluses. For example, its contribution to the state's fiscal income only took up 16.4% from 1950 to 1953. It appeared that it would not make great gains by expanding the state-owned monopoly property rights in agriculture. The second was to expand the state-owned property rights in light industry, particularly the consumer goods industry. However, since the rural population had accounted for 80% to 90% of the total population and the majority of the rural population suffered from the dual economy of poverty, the focus of light industry or the consumer goods industry would be restricted by the small market and insufficient demand (Lin Yifu et al., 1994, page 22). Therefore, it would be very slow for the state to gain the surplus by expanding property rights in light industry.

The state found not enough incentives to expand state-owned property rights in agriculture and light industry which show comparative advantages. Then why did the state finally choose heavy industry, of no comparative advantage but stricter constraints, as the object of expansion? It involves another key exogenous variable – that is, the external competition. When the state was encountered with direct threat by external competitors, it would necessarily allocate maximum economic resources and surplus to the sector that could cope with the threat.[3] At that time, the sector was exactly heavy industry (the output value of the heavy industry sector only occupied 7.9% of the total output value of industry and agriculture in 1949). It can be concluded that the Forging Ahead Strategy placing the priority to development of heavy industry as the core was the result of synthesis of the endogenous variable of the state pursuing expansion of the monopoly property rights and the exogenous variable of external competition. As the facts show, the monopoly property right form of the state had achieved rapid expansion through the Forging Ahead Strategy, and the state had its competitive power improved compared to the external competition and had also acquired a great amount of economic surplus. The integration of industrialization and the expansion of the monopoly property rights constituted a situation that deserves in-depth observation in economic history. According to statistics, the gross industrial output value in China had reached a growth rate of 23.3% on average from 1953 to 1960, and the proportion of the industrial output value in the gross agricultural and industrial output value increased from 43.1% in 1953 to 78.2% in 1960, while the proportion of the output value of heavy industry in the gross industrial output value also raised from 35.5%

to 66.6% in this period (Guo Kesha, 1993, pages 14–15). The proportion of industry in the national income had increased from 12.6% to 46.8% from 1949 to 1978, and the gross industrial output value in 1980 had grown by 17.9 times compared to 1952, with an annual average growth rate of 15.3% (Ma Hong, 1982, page 153).

IV   Constraint by the transaction costs and system of resource allocation

As the state had no other choice but to choose the economic growth strategy with heavy industry as the core and the corresponding foundation of the property rights was also rendered by nationalization, it seemed that specific implementation of the Forging Ahead Strategy could start under the circumstances. Nevertheless, as demonstrated by facts, the institutional framework of the state-owned property rights was not enough. In other words, nationalization was merely the necessary condition for implementation of industrialization, while the sufficient condition, in other words, the system of resource allocation adapted to the state-owned property right structure, needed to be created to step from the "design" to the "construction" of the Forging Ahead Strategy. The core issue lay in that factors required for the development of heavy industry such as capitals were subject to relative shortage in China, a backward country, which necessarily led to the expensive factor price. In such a case, industrialization was undoubtedly exposed to the severe constraint by the high cost. The natural response of the state was to design a system that could lower the factor price and reduce the cost of industrialization. In fact, the state had maintained very low prices of factors (such as low interest rate, low foreign exchange rate, low salaries and low price of energies and raw materials) and consumer goods from the 1950s to the reform.

Theoretically, despite the fact that nationalization was implemented and the monopoly structure of state-owned property rights was generated, if the transaction cost (such as the information and supervision cost) was a positive value, above low prices of factors and products would necessarily result in excess demand on these factors and products and thus raise the price, leading the state-owned enterprises to invest resources on the sectors of higher profitability (generally the sectors of comparative advantages). For example, in terms of taxes and profits achieved by each 100 Yuan, the light industry was 2.7 times the heavy industry in 1957 and even realized 3.1 times in 1980 (Li Yue et al., 1983). In regard to this, the state established a set of corresponding institutional arrangements in addition to the state-owned property right form (mainly state-owned enterprises) to assure that resources could be applied to the heavy industry preferred by the state and the state could control the maximum economic surplus. In this way, the mobilization and allocation of the surplus had been practically solved through internalization. It can be seen that the monopoly state-owned property right form could not eliminate the issue of transaction costs, but institutions are important in case of any transaction costs. Douglass North (1981) once believed that the governor (state) was universally faced with two constraints, the competition and the transaction costs (page 28). In China, the Forging Ahead Strategy was chosen largely based on the constraint by competition, while the system of resource allocation corresponding to the Forging Ahead Strategy was the product of the constraint by the transaction costs. According to research by Lin Yifu et al. (1997), it was the institutional arrangement of the lowest supervision costs (transaction costs) under the twisted macro-policy environment and highly concentrated system for state-owned enterprises to apply centralized fiscal control over the revenues and expenditures, with all profits turned in and all deficits cancelled upon verification (page 25). However, once the system was applied, the state-owned enterprises became pure "workshops" without independent capability in economic behaviors; since state-owned enterprises could not independently allocate human, fiscal and material resources or produce, supply and sell products, they had to follow external institutional arrangements to carry out these tasks. Therefore, a series of new institutional arrangements was set up, including the foreign trade and foreign exchange management system, the materials management system, the system of controlled procurement and distribution of agricultural products and the state-owned financial system that will be further discussed in this book.

4 Formation and evolution of state-owned financial institutional arrangements: conditions before reform

State-owned financial institutional arrangements were established as the supporting unit for state-owned enterprises to supply funds when the state was pursuing the monopoly property right form, which should share the similar logic of formation with the monopoly state-owned property rights. Surprisingly, distinguished from other state-owned property right forms, the state-owned financial property right form had no process of expansion in the first place but was practically about to be removed right from the formation of the monopoly financial property right form. However, since the reform, when other state-owned property right forms have been exposed to adjustments, reorganization and even relative contraction, the state-owned financial property right form has experienced rapid expansion. It can be seen that the state-owned financial property right form features its own logic in formation and evolution.

I The process of integration of financial property rights: a brief description

Generally speaking, the nationalization of banks in the early 1950s in China constituted an important step for the state to pursue the monopoly property right forms and had its process no different from nationalization of property rights of enterprises. Although the state had gradually controlled the financial process of China right after the foundation of new China, diversified financial property right forms still existed. In addition to the People's Bank of China controlled by the state, there were the privately owned Bank of China and Bank of Communications, joint public-private Xinhua Trust and Savings Bank, China Industrial Bank, Siming Commercial Savings Bank and Imperial Bank of China, insurance companies, several foreign-invested banks (such as HSBC and the Standard Chartered Bank, etc.) and numerous private old-style private banks. For example, China still had 833 private banks after reorganization by the end of 1949. The diversified financial property right forms had been rapidly integrated to be the single financial property right form monopolized by the state after 1952. For instance, the Bank of China had been designated as the specialized bank for foreign exchange of the state and merged with the Division of Foreign Affairs of the People's Bank of China (with only organizational system retained) in 1953; the Bank of Communications was incorporated into the People's Construction Bank of China under the Ministry of Finance due to its original businesses and cancelled in October 1954; the Agricultural Bank of China was only a bureau of the People's Bank of China; and domestic businesses of insurance companies were stopped in 1954. By the end of 1956, the state practically controlled the whole financial sector and private banks disappeared in China. Since then, the People's Bank of China, the only representative of the financial property rights of the state, became a special financial organization that released the currency and meanwhile provided specific financial businesses.

II   Functions of state-owned financial arrangements

A kind of special state-owned financial institutional arrangement was formed after integration of financial property rights. Generally speaking, this kind of institutional arrangement was established with state-owned enterprises as the principal part. As pointed out prior, the state had originally designed a set of institutional structures with the production process within the enterprise and resource allocation and product distribution outside the enterprise, so as to save the transaction costs, supervise the production process of state-owned enterprises and apply all economic surpluses to industrialization. For example, the means of production were supplied pursuant to the national plan; products were sold and allocated by the state in a unified way; revenues and expenditures were controlled by the state; profits and depreciation provisions of the enterprise were fully turned in to the state and incorporated in the state budget; the basic construction investment, fund for upgrading of fixed assets and technical transformation, trial production fee of new product and fee on procurement of sporadic fixed assets and some other funds needed by enterprises were provided through financial allocation by the state; the recruitment fee and salaries of enterprises were distributed according to the national plan; the circulating flows for enterprise production were also appropriated by the financial department according to the quota; and the seasonal and temporary circulating flows outside the quota were solved by the state-owned financial institutional arrangements (Lin Yifu et al., 1994, page 43). Evidently, the state built the state-owned financial institutions as the unit supplying funds to state-owned enterprises; in other words, the state-owned financial arrangement was the supporting institutional arrangement established by the state for the convenience of financing for state-owned enterprises (Zhang Jie, 1995b, page 56, 1996).

In view of this, it was not the state-owned financial arrangement itself which decided the quantity and method of the supply of financial resources. If these matters were decided by state-owned financial arrangements, the financial behaviors might be inconsistent with the utility function of the state. Therefore, soon after nationalization of financial property rights was basically completed in 1953, the People's Bank of China and its subordinate banks had set up the credit plan management organization to prepare and implement the comprehensive credit plan and apply the management system of centralized control over the revenues and expenditures in banks similar to the system in state-owned enterprises. Allocation of financial resources was conducted outside branches – for instance, all savings should be turned in to the head office and loans should be released from top to bottom based on the indicator verified by the head office, thus guaranteeing to allocate maximum financial resources to the "industrialization" of state-owned enterprises. Correspondingly, the state should also specify the prices of financial resources from top to bottom in accordance with the requirement on low cost of industrialization. For example, the monthly interest rate of the industrial credit loan in May 1950 was 3%, which was lowered to 2% by July 31, 1.5%–1.6% by April 1951, 0.6%–0.9% by January 1953 and the minimum 0.42% by 1971 (Zheng Xianbing, 1991, pages 115–120); the annual interest rate of the industrial loan of state-owned enterprises had maintained as 5.04% from October 1971 to 1980. As a matter of fact, the interest rate was frozen for two decades from 1958 to 1978 at a fixed level much lower than the average level (Yi Gang, 1996a, page 96). Theoretically, the interest rate should be a result of the equilibrium of demand and supply of financial resources, which was only available upon diversified property right forms in the market. Diversified property right forms had been integrated and fund supply and demand had been internalized during nationalization, when the logical result should be the failure of the adjustment by the interest rate, no matter how high or how low it was. In the case of the single property right form, resource allocation became an internal affair of state-owned property rights, and the interest rate showed nearly no significance because the inclination to over use the fund due to the interest rate of the loan lower than the opportunity cost or the shadow price of funds was avoided. Therefore, before discussing the financial repression by the low interest rate, the financial repression by the monopoly property right form should be first emphasized, since the former one was derived from the latter one.

As the quota of allocation of financial resources and the fund price were given, the financial functions of state-owned financial departments had been denied. Theoretically, financial functions of financial arrangements should be established upon the diversified structure of property rights and decentralized national savings, while the two conditions were exactly against the preference of the utility function of the state to pursue the monopoly property rights and centralized resources. In fact, after integration of property rights by the state, the economic contact of the whole society had been transformed from the external contact among different subjects of property rights to the internal contact among state-owned property rights. In this situation, the state-owned financial arrangements only played a role as the internal allocator of funds, and the internal allocation was practically a kind of financial allocation.

The denial of the financial function of financial arrangements might be relevant to the weak financing capability of state-owned banks at the early stage of industrialization. For instance, the total amount of ending assets of state-owned banks was 11.88 billion Yuan and the total amount of savings was 9.33 billion Yuan in 1952, respectively accounting for only 20.2% and 15.8% of the national income of the year (Lin Yifu et al., 1994, page 29). However, as discussed prior, the institutions left no room for the performance of financial functions after integration of property rights even if state-owned banks had great financing capability. The state created state-owned financial arrangements to restrict their financial functions. Only in this way could the utility function of financial arrangements be consistent with the utility function of the state.

Moreover, integration of property rights would be necessarily accompanied by centralized distribution of national income and direct control over economic surpluses by the state. For example, in 1978, the beginning of reform, savings of the state (or government) occupied 15.5% of GNP, while residents' savings only took up 1% of GNP (De Wulf & Goldsborough, 1986). As most investments relied on fund allocation by the government budget instead of financing through the banking system, the state-owned financial arrangements had barely any credit business other than passively providing some short-term loans to state-owned enterprises, and bank savings constituted their whole financial assets. State-owned financial arrangements seemed to have nothing to do.

Actually, the real function of state-owned financial arrangements was to provide a device to save the supervision cost of industrialization, for instance, by passively allocating financial resources and meanwhile supervising the fund use of state-owned enterprises to guarantee the compliance with the utility function of the state. Yi Gang (1996a) once believed that China had two currency flows before reform, cash flow and bank transfer flow. The former one was mainly about transactions among non-state-owned parties, while the latter one was for transactions among state-owned departments. State-owned enterprises were generally required to complete transactions through bank transfer and should not freely withdraw cash from their bank accounts. This principle was also applied to specialized banks and their branches, which should turn in most cash collected to the People's Bank of China and could keep only a small part to meet demands on liquidity. In this way, the convertible relation between cash and bank transfer was largely controlled by state-owned banks (page 23–24). Theoretically, the cash transactions among enterprises should be reduced to the minimum for convenience of supervision over state-owned enterprises, as the cost of enterprise supervision made the function of the volume of cash transactions.

III   An institutional arrangement that had been excluded

Since state-owned financial arrangements only played a role in supervision and hardly had any financial function, the financial institutional arrangements had been practically excluded from the set of institutional choices after integration of financial property rights. As institutional arrangements were "embedded" in the institutional structure, their efficiency was decided by how well other institutional arrangements could perform their functions, and each single institutional arrangement was intended to be the function of other institutional arrangements in the institutional structure. The set of institutional choices might be expanded or shrunk corresponding to changes to national policies, and the state might exclude certain institutional arrangements from the set of institutional choices for some reason (Lin Yifu, 2004). When having powerful control, the state could change the function or add new functions of certain institutional arrangement. In this situation, the institutional arrangement of originally low efficiency might gain the dominant position in the set of institutional choices, and the originally less important function might become the major function. It suggests that only when the set of institutional choices was exposed to changes due to disequilibrium of the institutional structure for some reason would state-owned financial institutional arrangements have their functions changed. Correspondingly, another important conclusion is that any effort to change the performance of financial arrangements by reforming any single state-owned financial arrangement or through transplanting would fail, no matter how attractive these efforts might seem. As one institutional arrangement constitutes the function of other institutional arrangements in the institutional structure, the change to one institutional arrangement is undoubtedly the function of changes to other institutional arrangements.

Here we could review the historical trace for state-owned financial institution to be excluded from the set of institutional choices. The People's Construction Bank of China was attached to the Ministry of Finance of China when founded in 1954, put under administration of the People's Bank of China in 1970 and finally transferred back to the Ministry of Finance in 1972. Surprisingly, the state had simply put the People's Bank of China under administration of the Ministry of Finance from 1969 to 1978 before the reform, while the People's Bank of China became a real institutional ghost and had only its name left but all organizations, personnel and businesses incorporated into the Ministry of Finance. Theoretically, the financial function of state-owned financial institutional arrangements disappeared along with integration of property rights, and supervision was raised to be the major function, but the financial function should be the irreplaceable function of financial arrangements, and comparatively the supervision function should be the replaceable function. Once the irreplaceable function was given up and only the replaceable function was remained for one institutional arrangement, the status of the institutional arrangement in the institutional structure would be extremely unstable.

It should be noted that that increment of state-owned financial property rights was not expanded, but their stock might be integrated or excluded at any time, which seemed to be inconsistent with the preference of the utility function of the state to expand the scale of property rights. As a matter of fact, the state was pursuing the expansion of aggregate property rights instead of individual property rights. The smaller scale of state-owned financial property right form enabled its better performance of the supervision function endowed by the state because the state also bears the responsibility to supervise the supervisor (state-owned banks).

Moreover, since not so many financial resources were available for allocation and funds were mostly internally distributed, the marginal cost of expansion of the financial property right form (including the organizational scale) would exceed the marginal income, making it not worthwhile. It indicated that when external financial resources demanding allocation increased and the marginal income of expansion of state-owned financial property rights started to grow, the state would automatically incorporate expansion of the boundary of state-owned financial property rights into its utility function, which has been demonstrated by the conditions after reform.

5   Expansion of the boundary of state-owned financial property rights: conditions after reform

I   About state concession

As the facts showed, the process of industrialization based on the monopoly property rights of the state was unsustainable. The fundamental cause lay in that the utility function of the state replacing the utility function of enterprises forced the state to pay extremely high information cost, leading to low efficiency of resource allocation, and led to the universal prominent issue of low efficiency of X. Therefore, the state had to announce concession ultimately after the low-efficiency growth for over two decades due to the dominance of state-owned property rights that was created by the state.

Generally speaking, the state concession was mainly attributed to the internal factor of state-owned property rights because the low efficiency of the economy gradually exposed the cost-benefit structure of the monopoly property right form to changes unfavorable to the state, that is, the low efficiency of the economy would ultimately affect the state's pursuit for maximum rent. In view of this, the state concession was internally produced by the utility function of the state. Another external reason that should not be ignored was that despite the low efficient industrialization for over two decades, the capability of the state to cope with external competitors (particularly the defense capability) had been significantly improved (the pressure from external competition was relatively released) since 1978, which resulted in corresponding changes to the utility function of the state.

II   Decentralization of financial resources and expansion of the boundary of state-owned financial property rights: process and nature

The structure of distribution of national income has been exposed to significant changes along with state concession after reform (the concession had been intermittently carried out several times before reform). In terms of the final status of distribution, the proportion of national income controlled by the state was lowered from 23.5% in 1978 to 11.7% in 1988, the national income of the enterprise sector showed small changes, and the proportion of the national income of residents was raised from 64.4% to 77.5% in this period. These results are calculated based on the broad sense of the national income. If the narrow sense of the national income is applied, the final distribution of the national income controlled by the state saw a greater decline, from 31.9% in 1978 to 12.2% in 1991, while the proportion of the national income of individuals grew from 56.5% to 75.3% in this period (Fan Yifei, 1994, page 270). These change to the structure of distribution of the national income indicated that the economic surplus was no longer subject to centralized control by the state but owned by the people in a decentralized way, which led to an important result, decentralization of financial resources. At the early stage of reform, the state was the major saver and investor, but since 1981, residents gradually replaced the state as the major owner of national savings. For example, residents' savings took up 23.55% in 1979 (compared to 42.8% of the government's savings and 33.65% of enterprises' savings); in 1981, the proportion of residents' savings (32.03%) exceeded the government's savings (22.29%) for the first time; and by 1996, the residents' savings occupied 83% of total savings (compared to 3% of the government's savings and 14% of enterprises' savings). The proportion of residents' savings in GNP also raised from 5.81% in 1978 to 56.82% in 1996.

The rapid change to the structure of the national income altered the preference of the state and urged the state to make efforts to adjust the structure of state-owned property rights, such as, importantly, increasing the proportion of the state-owned financial property right form. As a result, the financial institutional arrangements that had been excluded for a long time ushered in the opportunity of expansion again after reform and became the main path for the state to seek maximum utility. As the economic surplus acquired and controlled by the state through the fiscal channel suffered rapid decline due to economic reform, the original method of control and resource allocation of the economic surplus from top to bottom, mainly relying on national finance, no longer satisfied the requirement on maximum rent, so the state had to expand state-owned financial property rights to collect financial resources scattered among residents. The financial institutional arrangements embraced the comparative advantage in collecting scattered personal savings.

The expansion of state-owned financial institutional arrangements had been directly reflected by reconstruction of the organizational system. The People's Bank of China was separated from the Ministry of Finance in 1978, the Agricultural Bank of China and the People's Construction Bank of China were re-built in 1979, the Industrial and Commercial Bank of China was established to bear financial businesses originally undertaken by the People's Bank of China in 1983, the People's Bank of China then became the central bank in 1984, and the Bank of Communications held by the state was rebuilt in 1986 and so on; meanwhile, all state-owned banks were actively expanding their branches nationwide. In this way, a structure of state-owned financial property rights occupying a monopoly position was formed rapidly soon after reform was initiated. The reconstruction and expansion of the state-owned financial organizational system offered the condition for the state to continue to mobilize and control financial resources despite the rapid decline of the proportion of the government's savings and fiscal income.

Nevertheless, it is important to note that regardless of the expansion, state-owned financial institutional arrangements would always play a role as the replaceable arrangement of government finance under the dual structure, so the low efficiency of state-owned financial institutional arrangements was inevitable. For an example, from 1979 to 1996, among the capitals for production and investment of state-owned enterprises, those provided by state finance had increased from 63.877 billion Yuan to 145.9 billion Yuan, with an annual growth rate of 7.13%; those invested by state-owned banks had raised from 203.9 billion Yuan to 4,743.47 billion Yuan, with an annual growth rate of 123.69%. If assuming the sum of capitals invested by state finance and banks on state-owned enterprises as 1, the proportion of state finance had been lowered from 77.1% in 1979 to 15.4% in 1996, and the proportion of banks had been increased from 22.9% to 84.6%. At the same time, the capitals were reduced and the asset-liability ratio was increased for state-owned enterprises. The asset-liability ratio of state-owned enterprises was respectively 29.5% and 30% in 1979 and 1980, but the ratio went up to 40% after government appropriation being replaced by loans was performed in 1985, later to 60% in 1990, 75% in 1994 and about 78% in 1996.[4] Evidently, the higher dependence of capital investment of state-owned enterprises on banks reflected the greater control and dependence of the state on financial institutions rather than a rise in status of financial arrangements. In other words, the expansion of state-owned financial institutional arrangements only changed the internal structure of the state monopoly property right form. The state-owned financial arrangements still played a supporting role to state-owned enterprises, only with their significance sharply improved.

Notes

1 The role of ideology is ignored here. As a matter of fact, the state's pursuit for the monopoly property right involved the consideration of ideology, i.e., "abolishing private ownership and abolishing the system of exploitation", thus having reduced the cost of institutional innovation and won universal support of the society. Lin Yifu et al. (1997) believed that establishment of state ownership (ownership by the entire people) complied with the logic that the state controlled the economic surplus to support industrialization and meanwhile accorded with the ideology of communism. In other words, the state ownership of enterprises combined these three advantages from the respect of demand and supply and perfectly integrated the internal requirements of economic logic and rational improvements provided by the ideology, which might be of the lowest cost among all alternatives at that time (page 20).

2 Lin Yifu et al. once believed that private enterprises must be transformed to be state-owned enterprises to the maximum, in order to acquire the right to control the surplus and the accumulation direction and apply them to the development goal preferred by the state (1994, page 42). State-owned enterprises in China were not generated randomly, but were produced to serve the strategic goal of giving priority to development of heavy industry. After the traditional development strategy was chosen, it was necessary to implement nationalization of urban industry and commerce so that the state could control

the economic surplus and adapt the accumulation process to this strategic goal (1997, page 15).

3 The steel output of China in 1949 was 158,000 tons, compared to the steel output of 87.85 million tons in America, 27.33 million tons in the Soviet Union, 4.84 million tons in Japan, 12.12 million tons in the Federal Republic of Germany and 16.55 million tons in the UK.

4 See more details in Table 3.1 and Table 6.4.

2 Monetization and financial control by the state

The economic reform in China not only suggests diversification of property right forms and decentralization of financial resources, but also brings up the process of economic monetization (the proportion of transactions with the currency as medium in economic activities has been gradually increasing). Economic monetization alters the cost-benefit structure of financial control by the state. Compared to "internal" distribution of economic surplus through centralized control over the revenues and expenditures, monetization indicates "external" distribution, for instance, the control and distribution of the economic surplus is mainly realized through transaction. Therefore, monetization exerts complicated influences over the utility function for a state exposed to the centrally planned economy for the long term. As is known to us, the state, acting as a rational economic agent, pursues both the maximum control over rent and economic surplus and the minimum cost of control, while establishment of the monopoly property right form guarantees realization of this goal. Before the factor of monetization was introduced, the cost of state control was often considered a constant due to unitary monopoly of the property rights. The currency itself was merely a symbol of value and measurement unit and was neutral in deciding the control cost. The neutral characteristic of the currency was also expected by the state pursuing the monopoly property right structure. As shown in the discussion on functions of state-owned financial arrangements in Chapter 1, Section 4, Point II, the state attempted to reduce the use of cash currencies as the medium to the minimum in economic activities through the two separate currency processes, because the cost of control by the state is the increasing function of the scale of economic activities with the currency as the medium. Evidently, the low monetization level better satisfies the utility function of the state and shows a certain internal logic connection with the exclusion of state-owned financial institutional arrangements. Only after the currency was no longer exposed to separate treatment and became the common medium of economic activities would the significance of financial institutional arrangements be highlighted. However, the state needs to pay increasingly greater cost for control if it sticks to the previous control method as economic monetization is gradually improved.

Nevertheless, it is interesting that economic reform starting from a low level of monetization would show certain special advantages, for instance, a comparatively long monetization interval, where the capability to absorb and dilute money would be extremely strong due to the huge potential money demand in the economy of low monetization. Under these circumstances, the state could invest a certain amount of money on the economy without worrying about inflation, which means that the state would acquire great benefits from monetization. On this basis, although monetization would increase the control cost, it also would provide internal incentives to push the state to boost monetization. When the increase of the control cost of the state brought by monetization is smaller than the benefits from monetization, the state would actively promote economic monetization and meanwhile would design and control financial arrangements that could effectively acquire monetization benefits.

1 Monetization interval and monetization benefits

I The Mystery of China: low inflation and high financial growth

Since the reform, finance in China has practically grown at a surprising rate but has avoided high inflation. The money stock (M2) of China reached an average growth rate of 25.2% between 1978 and 1996, while the average growth rate of GNP in the same period reached 9.7% and the index of retail prices had risen by 6.82% on average. At the same time, monetization has reached as high as 108.58% in 1996 in China, compared to 59% in the US, 104% in the UK, 114% in Japan, 70% in Germany, 40% in Indonesia, 44% in South Korea, 89in of Malaysia and 79% in Thailand in 1995.

Professor Ronald Mckinnon (1996), an American economist, had conducted detailed comparative research on the process of marketization in China, Eastern Europe and the Commonwealth of the Independent States (CIS). The result showed that the CIS, Eastern Europe and China had all suffered rapid fiscal decline during marketization. For example, the proportion of fiscal income in GNP in Russia was approximately 40% upon dissolution of the Soviet Union and was lowered to about 20% in 1993 (even to below 20% in 1995), and the proportion of the Chinese fiscal income in GNP sharply declined from 34.8% in 1978 to 18.5% in 1991 (even to below 20% in 1995 and 10.87% in 1996).[1] However, only China has successively inhibited inflation. According to the sequence of economic marketization proposed by Mckinnon, financial growth must be established upon the fiscal balance of the central government, otherwise the growth would be contained by following inflation. Therefore, he regarded China maintaining stable prices and high financial growth at the same time while suffering fiscal decline as the "Mystery of China" (page 271).

II Initial conditions and monetization interval

Differences among China, the CIS and Eastern Europe during marketization have a direct relationship with their own special initial conditions.[2] The most evident difference lay in the monetization level when the reform was initiated. According to statistics of an authoritative development report released by the World Bank (1996a), the M2/GDP of the Soviet Union in 1990 reached 100%, while the value of China in 1978 was only 25% (page 21).[3] It demonstrates that the Soviet Union had been monetized at the beginning of the reform, but Chinese economy saw a low level of monetization.

Low monetization of the economy at the initial stage of reform enabled synchronous advance of institutional evolution and economic monetization and thus avoided the "inflation trap". The huge cost was needed for economic reform itself, which was paid through investment of money at the initial stage of reform since no corresponding reform benefit was acquired, thus leading to the possibility of inflation. In comparison, the economy of low monetization could absorb and dilute money. As mentioned prior, between 1978 and 1996, the money stock had been growing much faster than the economy and prices in China, suggesting a huge amount of excess money supply. According to calculations, the excess rate reached 8.68% – that is, M2 had grown by 25.2% (9.7% of growth of GNP + 6.82% of rise of prices); if the nominal GNP was converted to real GNP, the rate would go beyond 10%. By 1996, the excess rate reached 11.35% (People's Bank of China, 1997). Such a high excess money supply did not lead to high inflation, evidently because a considerable part (if not the whole) had been absorbed and diluted by the economy of low monetization. It is estimated that the money supply should be increased by 6% to 8% each year to satisfy the demand of the newly monetized economy on money at the early stage of reform (Huang Xiaoxiang, 1988).

III   Gains from currency release and financial surplus

As the money was exposed to excess supply without too much pressure on inflation, a great sum of gains from currency release would be generated in China. As estimated by some Chinese scholars, the gains occupied approximately 3% of GNP on average between 1978 and 1992 (Yi Gang, 1996b); according to another estimate, they accounted for 5.4% of GNP on average between 1986 and 1993, and the total amount of currency release in this period reached 844.72 billion Yuan (Xie Ping, 1996, page 41); the World Bank (1996a, page 35) even believed that the maximum amount in 1993 attained about 11% of GDP (generally 1% to 2% in countries of the market economy). The huge amount of gains from currency release rendered the timely and strong support to the central fiscal condition in decline and the state-owned economy in difficulties and low efficiency, therefore relieved the reform resistance, and particularly intensified the reform incentives to the state, the reform pusher.

The gains from currency release only made up a part of total incomes from the whole process of monetization. Despite the large amount, the gains from currency release were obviously insufficient to offset the reform cost of a huge economy and support the economic growth, let alone that the currency release was subject to strict constraint by the gradually improving monetization level. As monetization approached 100%, the gains from currency release would decrease progressively. In this situation, it would necessarily lead to high inflation if relying on gains from currency release for the long term. In other words, the monetization and high financial growth in China would end up in the "trap of inflation". However, this situation has not shown up in the whole process of reform. Despite several times of severe price rises in China after 1984, the conditions had all been successfully restored. Undoubtedly, there have been some other incomes in addition to gains from currency release.

As a matter of fact, monetization in China has been providing a considerable amount of financial surplus to the economy from the very beginning. We first noticed that the institutional changes in the rural area, which symbolized the start of monetization, had significantly improved trade conditions in the rural area, promoted the rapid growth of agricultural output and vigorously increased the cash flow in the rural area; along with the rise of incomes, farmers started to accumulate cash and save money in banks. Same as the loan applied by the central bank to the state, the cash accumulation had become a part of gains from currency release, as mentioned prior. By comparison, savings had been growing at a higher rate and reached an annual average growth rate of 41% between 1979 and 1984. The loan resources of the banking system of the state had been accumulated and expanded through the farmers' financial assets with savings as the main form, but meanwhile the direct loans of the state to the rural area were fewer. From 1979 to 1984, the total amount of loans issued by rural credit cooperatives (representing the state) to farmers, township and village enterprises and collective farming only accounted for 33.9% of savings on average, which only rose to 66.8% even by 1991 (Qian, 1993). Therefore, in the key period at the beginning of reform, Chinese farmers, accounting for over three-quarters of the total population, had surprisingly contributed financial surpluses to other economic sectors as net lenders (Ronald Mckinnon, 1996, page 277).

When the reform was carried out in the urban area and the industry sector, the scale of financial surpluses had rapidly expanded. As shown in Table 2.2, urban residents' savings had maintained rapid growth since the reform. The proportion of total residents' savings in GNP, consisting of urban and rural residents' savings, was only 5.6% in 1978, but had seen a constant rise and reached 56.82% in 1996 (compared to gross domestic product, GDP). Undoubtedly, urban residents' savings had been provided to the state as financial surpluses through the state-owned banking system. Non-state-owned economies had particularly attained rapid growth during the reform, but they failed to acquire vigorous financial support from state-owned banks when they gradually became the major contributor to economic growth. For example, non-state-owned economies only took up 22.4% of the gross value of industrial output in 1978, compared to 69.1% in 1995; the contribution rate of non-state-owned sectors to budgetary revenues increased from 18% in 1980 to 39.4% in 1993; and the employment ratio of non-state-owned sectors (including agriculture) had maintained above 80% for a long time. However, the amount of industrial loans used by non-state-owned economies only occupied approximately 20% of the total amount. According to Table 2.1, the average proportion of loans used by non-state-owned sectors (including township and village enterprises and agriculture) in all bank loans between 1985 and 1996 was only

Table 2.1 Shares of loans to non-state-owned sectors by financial organizations in China between 1985 and 1996

				(%)		
Year	*Urban collective*	*Urban individual*	*Township enterprise*	*Sino-foreign or foreign-funded enterprise*	*Agriculture*	*All non-state-owned sectors*
1985	4.95	0.17	5.63		6.85	17.60
1986	5.11	0.13	6.82		6.68	18.94
1987	5.47	0.16	7.25		7.28	20.16
1988	5.58	0.17	7.59		7.19	20.53
1989	5.15	0.11	7.39		7.12	19.97
1990	4.93	0.09	7.42		7.17	19.61
1991	4.74	0.08	7.63		7.39	19.84
1992	5.77	0.26	7.16		7.54	20.73
1993	5.96	0.33	8.22		6.47	20.98
1994	5.08	0.38		1.94	11.38	18.78
1995	4.26	0.39		1.98	5.99	12.62
1996	4.31	0.46		2.20	11.65	18.62

Data source: The data of 1985–1991 is introduced from Ronald Mckinnon (1996), Table 13.9; and the data of 1992–1996 is calculated based on relevant data in the *China Financial Outlook (1994–1997)*.

Note: The shares of loans of agriculture incorporated the loans for township enterprises and undertakings after 1994.

19.03%, while the highest proportion was merely 20.98% in 1993. It suggests that state-owned economies could borrow a large amount of financial surpluses from non-state-owned sectors so that the government could provide sufficient funds to meet the demands of state-owned enterprises and central financial needs without collecting high inflation tax and implementing reform of the tax system.

2   Issue of "powerful financial capacity"

I   An institutional replacement

As mentioned prior, monetization in China has supplied incomes from currency release and financial surpluses to economies in reform and enabled the state to successfully offset the quick fiscal decline. However, other than incomes from currency release, financial surpluses (particularly the large amount of money savings of residents) were distributed in an extremely decentralized way, and corresponding institutional arrangements must be established to transfer them to be funds available to the state. There are two kinds of institutional arrangements to acquire financial surpluses theoretically: the tax system and the financial system. Evidently, China has not applied an efficient approach to acquire financial surpluses through the tax system until now. In particular, although individuals have been occupying an increasing proportion of the national income since the reform, the system of collecting personal income tax has not been correspondingly set up. For example, urban and rural personal incomes occupied 50% of GNP in 1978, which approached 70% by 1995; but personal income taxes in 1995 only accounted for 0.2% of GNP, compared to 10% in the UK and the US, 7.1% in France, 9.3% in Germany and 1.2% in India in 1992, as well as 3.6% in South Korea in 1993. In 1994, personal income taxes in China only took up 1.5% of total taxes, while the average value was 28% for industrial countries and 11% for developing countries (World Bank, 1996b, page 38). By comparison, state-owned financial institutions that had gained rapid expansion since the reform have maintained strong capability in gathering financial surpluses. According to statistics, urban and rural residents' savings grew at an annual average rate of 35% between 1978 and 1996, while the total amount of savings increased from 21.06 billion Yuan in 1978 to 3,852.08 billion Yuan in 1996 and further increased to over 4.8 trillion by March 1998. The vast majority of these savings (such as 92.5% of urban savings in 1996) were controlled by the state through accounts of state-owned banks. It can be seen that financial institutions had replaced part of the functions of the tax system in mobilizing financial resources (surpluses). In the later process of allocation of financial resources, financial institutions replaced part of the functions of the fiscal system. As proved by facts, the replacement was not only the key to the success of reform but also the origin leading to difficulties of reform in the future.

II Weak treasury and "powerful financial capacity"

Against the fact of decline of the fiscal capacity of the central government since the reform, the judgment of China having a "weak government" was once proposed by someone in the theoretical realm (Wang Shaoguang & Hu Angang, 1996, pages 12–42), thus bringing about a fierce academic debate. I do not intend to get involved in the debate, but only try to state that China has a "weak government" indeed from the aspect of central fiscal capacity. From 1953 to 1983, central fiscal revenue accounted for 22.6% of the gross fiscal revenue on average (Zhang Fengbo, 1988, page 179). Since the reform, the proportion of central fiscal revenue in the gross fiscal revenue had ups and downs, rising before 1985 when the maximum proportion once approached 50%, declining slowly afterwards and dropping to below 40% in 1991, slightly rising again in 1992 (International Monetary Fund, 1995, page 28, Figure 6) and reaching approximately 40% in 1996. If the extra-budgetary funds controlled by local governments (compared to budgetary funds, the proportion of extra-budgetary funds increased from 8.4% in 1978 to 30.3% in 1993, and, if the treasury of villages and townships was considered, the proportion should be 40%) were incorporated, the ratio of the central fiscal revenue would be lowered to one-fifth, while the central treasury in most countries occupied over 60% (such as 88% in France, 63% in Germany, 85% in the UK, 69% in India, 84% in Brazil and 83% in Mexico). However, China also has a "powerful government" from the respect of the financial capability of the central government. In addition to the strong capability of state-owned banks in mobilizing financial surpluses, the major four state-owned specialized banks still occupied a market share of about 75% in 1996 despite slow decline since the reform (People's Bank of China, 1997, page 38); meanwhile, finance (particularly state-owned finance) had rendered huge funds to public deficits of the state and business subsidies, and, for an example, the average deficits of the public sector took up 11.16% of GDP while the financing by banking sectors occupied 8.2% of GDP; and the state still maintained great capability in controlling other economic areas through financial measures, which could be demonstrated by the great results of macro financial control since 1984, particularly between 1993 and 1996 (People's Bank of China, 1997). Therefore, it is biased to reach the conclusion of "weak government". To be more accurate, the state capacity of China can be concluded as the weak treasury and "powerful financial capacity". Basic conditions are shown in Table 2.2.

It shall be noticed that collocation of weak treasury and "powerful financial capacity" makes a factor contributing to the success of reform in China, but it can only be realized in the special monetization interval in China. It suggests that the collocation could hardly be maintained when monetization reaches a certain level (such as 100%). To be more specific, if the government fails to become more powerful at that time and the factor that supports the "powerful financial capacity" disappears, it would necessarily lead to inflation if the state continues to rely on financial institutions.

3 Financial control by the state and difficult choices of state-owned financial institutions

I Financial control by the state: description

Evidently, the phenomenon of "powerful financial capacity" has been directly relevant to financial control by the state since the very beginning. The structure of national savings of China has been exposed to great changes (refer to relevant discussions in Chapter 1, Section 5, Point II) after reform, as the proportion of individuals, enterprises and governments respectively changed from 23.55%, 33.65% and 42.8% in 1979 to 83%, 14% and 3% in 1996. A state-owned financial system controlled by the state and holding the monopoly status was demanded, in order to effectively collect the rapidly growing individual savings for the state to make up the decline of the proportion of government savings. It was also necessary to restrict residents' choices on financial assets so that more residents' savings could directly flow to accounts at state-owned banks. As the facts showed, the state achieved the intended purpose through these control measures. For instance, residents' financial assets in 1991 consisted of 19.16% of cash, 70.1% of savings and 10.74% of securities and insurances. As it should be, the state had successfully maintained the incentives to savings with positive interest rates to assure residents' high inclination to savings, such as the interest rate indexation applied upon relatively high inflation rate in particular. In this way, residents' savings had been pouring into financial institutions, mainly state-owned banks, due to residents'

Table 2.2 Pattern of "weak treasury" and "powerful financial capacity" in China

			(%)							
Year	(1) Proportion of the fiscal revenue in GNP (excluding incomes from debts)	(2) Proportion of the central fiscal revenue in GNP (including incomes from debts)	(3) Proportion of deficits of public sectors in GDP				(4) Proportion of residents' savings in GNP	(5) Proportion of financial sources to subsidies to state-owned enterprises		
			Total amount	Government budget	State-owned enterprises	Among which: bank financing		Total amount	Treasury	Finance
1978	31.2	–	–	−0.28	–	–	5.6	–	–	–
1979	26.7	–	–	5.15	–	–	7.03	–	–	–
1980	23.3	–	–	3.81	–	–	8.94	–	–	–
1981	21.3	4.7	–	2.07	–	–	10.97	–	–	–
1982	20.0	5.0	–	2.18	–	–	13.01	–	–	–
1983	20.1	6.4	–	2.11	–	–	15.36	–	–	–
1984	20.5	7.5	–	1.75	–	–	17.45	–	–	–
1985	20.8	8.3	–	0.80	–	–	18.96	9.9	7.5	2.4
1986	21.9	9.5	–	2.15	–	–	23.08	9.9	7.5	2.4
1987	19.5	8.0	10.7	2.1	8.6	8.4	27.19	10.2	7.2	3.0
1988	16.8	7.4	10.7	2.4	8.3	8.1	27.02	7.0	6.4	0.6
1989	16.7	6.9	11.4	2.3	9.1	8.9	32.18	6.9	6.9	−0.1
1990	16.3	7.6	12.3	2.2	10.1	10.3	39.75	6.2	6.4	−0.2
1991	14.57	7.0	10.9	2.5	8.5	8.7	42.75	5.8	5.2	0.6
1992	13.08	–	13.1	2.6	10.5	8.2	44.14	7.5	3.9	3.6
1993	12.56	–	12.7	2.3	10.3	9.8	43.90	6.3	3.1	3.2
1994	11.19	–	9.9	1.7	8.2	5.7	46.16	3.9	2.2	1.7

(Continued)

Table 2.2 (Continued)

	(1) Proportion of the fiscal revenue in GNP (excluding incomes from debts)	(2) Proportion of the central fiscal revenue in GNP (including incomes from debts)	(3) Proportion of deficits of public sectors in GDP (%)				(4) Proportion of residents' savings in GNP	(5) Proportion of financial sources to subsidies to state-owned enterprises		
Year			Total amount	Government budget	State-owned enterprises	Among which: bank financing		Total amount	Treasury	Finance
1995	10.71	5.6	8.7	1.7	7.0	5.7	50.91	–	–	–
1996	10.87	–	–	–	–	–	56.82	–	–	–

Data source and note: Column (1): The data between 1978 and 1990 is introduced from Wang Shaoguang and Hu Angang (1996); the data between 1991 and 1996 is calculated based on Table 3.1 of *1997 China Financial Outlook*, which should be the ratio of the fiscal revenue to CDP.

Column (2): The data is introduced from Wang Shaoguang and Hu Angang (1996), and the data of 1995 is estimated.

Column (3): The data is introduced from Table 1.4 of the World Bank (1996b) and the data of 1995 is estimated; the data of the government budget between 1978 and 1986 is introduced from Wang Shaoguang and Hu Angang (1996), which should be the ratio of the fiscal deficit to GNP.

Column (4): The data between 1978 and 1990 is calculated according to Figure 1.1 and Table 4.2 of Yi Gang (1996a), and the data on residents' savings is from the state-owned banking system; and the data between 1991 and 1996 is calculated based on Table 3.1 and Table 3.9 of *1997 China Financial Outlook*, which should be the ratio of residents' savings to GDP.

Column (5): The data is introduced from Table 2.1 of World Bank (1996b).

trust in the state-owned banking system and relative shortage of financial assets. The system of financial resource allocation with state-owned banks as the principal had been therefore formed, as residents' massive amounts of savings had flowed into accounts of financial institutions (particularly the state-owned banks). According to statistics, savings and loans of banks and financial institutions still occupied as high as 83% of total financial assets by 1995 despite their slow decline since the reform. This is clearer through international comparison. Statistics of the World Bank (World Bank, 1996a) indicated that the ratio of bank assets in China (only including state-owned banks and rural credit cooperatives) to CDP in 1993 was 128%, much higher than the ratio of stocks and bonds of 20%. By comparison, the two ratios were respectively 69% and 84% in South Korea, 93% and 396% in Malaysia, 51% and 117% in the Philippines and 95% and 112% in Thailand, where the ratios of stocks and bonds were all higher than those of bank assets. It was also the similar situation in Japan, Germany, the UK and the US, while two ratios for these four countries were respectively 143.25% and 149% on average.

The great amount of financial resources put together in state-owned banks made it convenient for the state to apply these resources in light of its preference. Since state-owned banks are owned by the state, they have to undertake the financing obligations handed over by the state (government). As a matter of fact, each state-owned bank provided so-called policy-related loans to many key projects and social welfare projects of the government in varying degrees. These loans accounted for 18% of the total amount of loans of the Industrial and Commercial Bank of China, 22% of the Bank of China, 48% of the Agricultural Bank of China and 53% of the People's Construction Bank of China, with an average proportion reaching 35.25% in 1992 (IMF, 1995, page 36). Nevertheless, the pattern of interest pursuit of state-owned banks had been exposed to significant changes along with the advancing reform, and they started seeking private interests in addition to the scope of interest of the state. Meanwhile, under the influence of decentralization reform, local interest preference had been incorporated in the function of interest pursuit of the state. In this case, the state had carried out strict control over the credit scale and the corresponding mechanism of a large amount of reserves in state-owned banks to restrict the interest pursuit inconsistent with the state preference. In 1984 when the People's Bank of China and the Industrial and Commercial Bank of China were set up in a smaller unit, it was provided that specialized banks should submit 40% of general savings, 25% of rural savings, 20% of enterprise savings and 100% of fiscal deposits to the People's Bank of China as the deposit reserves. In this way, the state controlled approximately 40%–50% of all credit funds nationwide. After times of adjustments, the reserve ratio of general savings is still as high as 13% now. Moreover, specialized banks are required to hand in 5%–11% as the excess reserves. Therefore, the gross ratio of legal reserves reaches as high as 18%–24% (Figure 2.1). By comparison, the gross ratio of legal reserves of financial organizations in Western countries is generally below 10%, such as 10% in the US, 0.5% in the UK, 2.5% in Switzerland and 1.3% in Japan in 1992. As proved by facts, the mechanism of a large amount of reserves has exerted restrictions over the power of state-owned banks to independently apply the funds

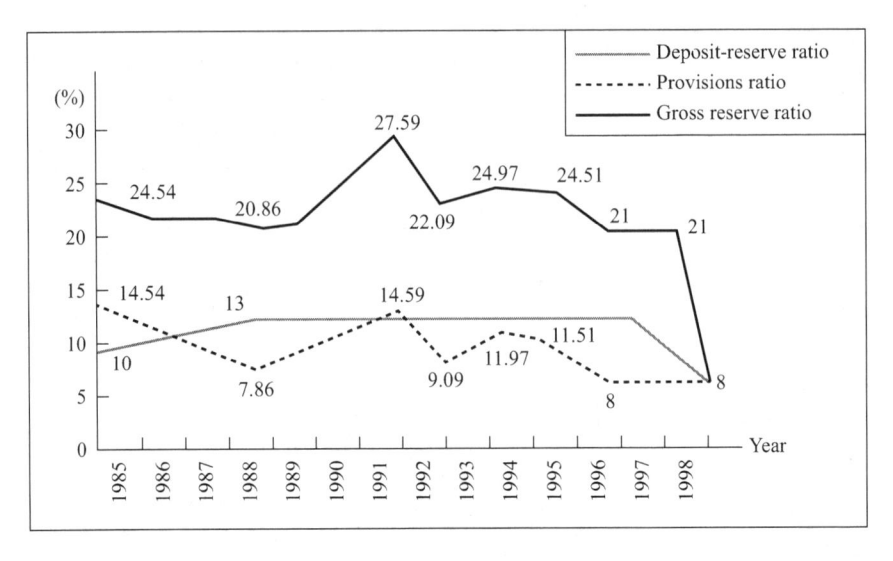

Figure 2.1 Changes to the reserve ratio in China: 1985–1998

and has strengthened the dominance and control on financial resources by the state. Interestingly, although the central bank has been providing excessive credits to specialized banks, with the excessive credits reaching 662.3 billion Yuan by the end of 1994, most re-loans given by the central bank to specialized banks are applied to special purposes. The increase of funds to specialized banks brought about by the excessive credits could not make up the loss of the funds management right of specialized banks due to submission of reserves (Xie Ping, 1996, page 38).

II Two controls: before and after 1988

Gains from monetization would undoubtedly decrease along with the rising level of monetization. According to the research of Yi Gang (1996a), the Chinese economy exposed to new monetization between 1979 and 1984 had absorbed a huge amount of excessive money supply, so the inflation rate was low and the state had acquired great monetary gains. After 1985, as monetization obviously slowed down, the excessive money supply mainly resulted in inflation, and the corresponding gains from monetization also decreased (pages 132 and 152). Xie Ping (1996) believed that conflicts among stakeholders got increasingly prominent since the economic reform was carried out in a deeper level after 1992, leading to huge demand on subsidies to the system reform. However, the gains from currency issue available as subsidies to the system reform were far from enough because economic monetization had reached the highest level. The government had to resort to expanding bank loans and currency issue for benefit compensation to cope with various conflicts, which caused the fiercer inflation (page 43). Based on the analysis of the World Bank (1996a), although looking like it was impossible to meet the demands of enterprises and residents, China had maintained rapid economic growth while avoiding inflation by relying on cash and bank deposits at the early stage of reform. However, the monetary demands would not last long since the monetary balance had reached a high level and even approached GDP in 1994. Other substitutive forms to bank deposits have been increasing, such as equities, enterprise bonds, foreign exchanges and real properties, which, in addition to the public application of funds, would directly transform the deficits incurred by financing of the state from public sectors through banks to inflation. Although the central government is still able to control inflation through regular adjustment by administrative control, its efficiency will be gradually lowered (page 35). Ronald Mckinnon (1996) believed that monetization of the Chinese economy had attained 97% by 1991 and that the government should not completely rely on borrowings of state-owned banks any longer, otherwise the great economic performance achieved in the previous 13 years would be in danger and the inflation that once took place in Eastern Europe might turn up again (page 291).

The turning point and time for increase and decrease of gains from monetization are discussed prior, which is of great significance in unveiling the nature of financial control by the state. We have noticed that when gains from monetization were increasing, financial control by the state was generally active, and when gains from monetization were exposed to gradual decline after the turning point, financial control would become passive if the economic system had not been successfully transformed. To be specific, at the beginning of reform, gains from monetization had risen sharply. As the state-owned financial system holding the monopoly status at that time was the most convenient tool to accumulate these gains, the state spontaneously had incentives to control finance in order to effectively mobilize and allocate the gains. However, the state-owned economic sector that used the gains failed to carry out transformation along with the further development of the reform. The demand on interest subsidies of this sector was increasing despite the gradual rise of monetization level and decrease of gains from monetization. Consequently, the expansion of currency release by the state led to inflation. The state began to be aware of the rising risk in financial control. But since the market economy system undertaking coordination and reorganization of risks has not been established, the rising pressure of inflation resulted in increasing urgency in financial control and the smaller possibility for the state to exit control (or change the method of control).

As shown in Table 2.3, monetization had been advancing in China before the reform after all, growing from 14.88% in 1952 to 36.35% in 1977. The low monetization level actually reflected the immature economic development, which accidentally rendered an important condition for successful development of the economic reform at the earlier stage of the reform in China.

Then where is the turning point for the active financial control of the state to become passive? According to Table 2.4 and Figure 2.2, after growing for 10 consecutive years after reform, the monetization index (M2/GNP) of the Chinese

Table 2.3 Monetization of China: conditions before the reform

Year	M2 (billion Yuan)	GDP (billion Yuan)	M2/GDP (%)
1952	10.13	68.09	14.88
1953	11.37	81.96	13.87
1954	13.24	86.47	15.31
1955	14.59	91.09	16.02
1956	17.50	101.96	17.16
1957	19.77	104.96	18.84
1958	31.32	129.24	24.23
1959	39.17	141.26	27.73
1960	40.91	141.03	29.01
1961	43.98	115.13	38.20
1962	43.62	106.81	40.84
1963	43.66	115.60	37.77
1964	43.47	134.79	32.25
1965	49.76	160.34	31.03
1966	56.63	183.34	30.89
1967	62.97	171.89	36.63
1968	66.69	163.57	40.77
1969	65.92	186.92	35.27
1970	65.11	222.65	29.24
1971	71.49	240.10	29.78
1972	75.49	246.92	30.57
1973	87.03	267.96	32.48
1974	93.68	271.43	34.51
1975	101.75	290.10	35.07
1976	108.46	281.29	38.56
1977	110.73	304.64	36.35

Data source: The data in this table is calculated based on Table 4.2 of Yi Gang (1996a) and Table 2.6 of Zhang Fengbo (1988).

Table 2.4 Monetization, inflation and economic growth of China: 1978–1996

	(%)		
Year	M2/GNP	Inflation rate	GDP growth
1978	31.98	0.7	11.7
1979	36.11	2.0	7.6
1980	40.79	6.0	7.8
1981	45.97	2.4	4.5
1982	48.85	1.9	8.7

	(%)		
Year	*M2/GNP*	*Inflation rate*	*GDP growth*
1983	51.63	1.5	10.3
1984	57.53	2.8	14.7
1985	57.84	8.8	13.5
1986	65.88	6.0	8.8
1987	69.85	7.3	11.6
1988	67.68	18.5	11.3
1989	70.63	17.8	4.1
1990	82.23	2.1	3.8
1991	89.91	2.9	9.2
1992	95.31	5.4	14.2
1993	91.15	13.2	13.5
1994	100.92	21.7	12.6
1995	105.38	14.8	10.2
1996	108.58	6.1	9.7

Data source: The data in this table is calculated based on Yi Gang (1996a, 1996b) and *China Financial Outlook (1994–1997)*.

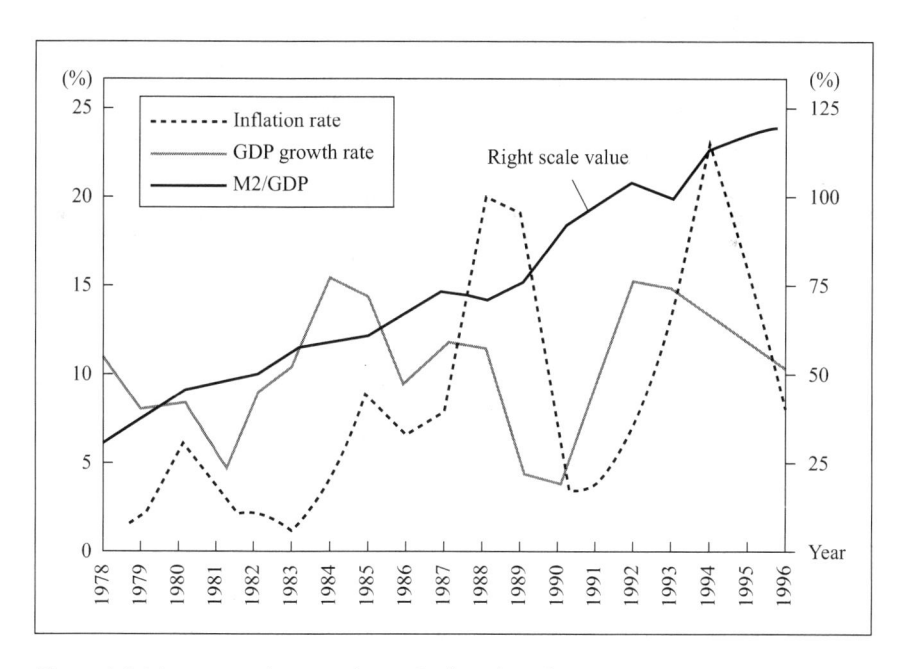

Figure 2.2 Monetary and economic trends since the reform

economy saw the first decline in 1988, from 69.85% in the prior year to 67.68% while in the same year, the rate of inflation (18.5%) exceeded the growth rate of GDP (11.3%) for the first time. Despite the short duration of the process, it symbolized the change of gains from monetization from increase to decrease. Since then, economic operation and reform in China have been exposed to alteration of expansion and contraction, manifested by the relaxing and tightening of financial control by the state. It indicated that financial control of the state had changed from active to passive since the year 1988. The monetization index dropped again from 95.31% in 1992 to 91.15% in 1993, with the decreasing rate reaching 4.16%, larger than that at the first time of decline. It demonstrates that the decline of gains from monetization has accelerated. It can be predicted that the decreasing rate of the monetization index would be higher next time and that state control would be harder if there is no substantial improvement of the state-owned economic system. Therefore, we could reach a conclusion that the turning point (1985) mentioned by Yi Gang was too early and the turning point (around 1992) proposed by Xie Ping et al. was too late.

III   The return and cost of financial control by the state: empirical evidence

The basic trend of financial control by the state since the reform is revealed in the prior discussions. To describe and understand the trend more accurately, it is necessary to investigate the return-cost structure of financial control by the state. The first difficulty encountered is how to select and confirm the factors of the return and cost of financial control by the state and the second is how to acquire the corresponding data. Even after having completed the arduous process of screening, we still hold some doubts about reliability of these factors. The factors of the return of financial control by the state initially determined consist of (1) incomes from currency release, (2) tax contributions from state-owned finance and (3) financial support to the state-owned economy. The former two are regarded as the direct return and (3) is the indirect return. By comparison, the data on the direct return can be easily acquired, but the data on the indirect return cannot be directly acquired, so the financed amount provided by state-owned banks to the deficits of the public sector is applied as the approximate value for calculation. The factors of the cost of financial control by the state include (1) operating costs of state-owned financial institutions, (2) the savings interest provided by state-owned financial institutions, (3) the cost of supervision by the central bank (with the operating cost of the central bank as the basis) and (4) the loss incurred by the low efficiency of allocation of financial resources by state-owned banks. The former three constitute the direct cost and the data can be directly acquired. Item (4) is the indirect cost, which is represented with the estimate value of bad debts of state-owned banks. The calculation result of the return and cost of financial control by the state is shown in Table 2.5. It is important to point out that we have tried our best to apply the authoritative statistics for relevant data in Table 2.5 and have to

Table 2.5 The return and cost of financial control by the state

					(Billion Yuan)				
Year	R_m				C_m				
	SE	BT	FS	Total	MC	SC	SI	BD	Total
1979	5.461	0.615	11.897	17.973	0.432		1.113	2.812	4.357
1980	7.406	0.189	24.928	32.523	0.525		2.157	7.872	10.554
1981	4.883	0.217	21.031	26.131	0.762		2.828	1.829	5.419
1982	4.210	2.367	21.851	28.428	1.025		3.890	4.440	9.355
1983	8.936	2.562	21.756	33.254	1.166		5.141	1.943	8.250
1984	25.516	11.529	25.416	63.461	1.778		6.997	0.203	8.978
1985	106.425	25.074	30.869	162.368	2.071	1.145	11.099	1.286	15.601
1986	44.340	30.114	48.415	122.869	3.656	1.924	16.111	9.027	30.718
1987	27.959	34.117	94.979	157.055	5.135	2.447	22.128	85.000	114.710
1988	72.574	33.630	114.001	220.205	7.032	3.816	32.845	111.000	154.693
1989	71.307	19.956	142.379	233.042	7.652	4.468	58.366	156.000	226.486
1990	132.223	39.015	182.117	353.355	8.112	5.190	60.775	174.000	248.077
1991	136.054	28.921	188.075	353.050	9.891	6.600	69.866	186.200	272.557
1992	129.981	24.828	218.432	373.241	13.249	8.836	88.890	300.000	410.975
1993	247.350	36.260	339.417	623.027	16.742	13.130	166.934	650.000	846.806
1994	279.376	13.579	265.770	558.725	32.209	23.419	236.276	700.000	991.904
1995	215.157	30.910	332.085	578.152	41.646	28.234	325.692	800.000	1,195.572
1996	620.170	37.503	406.770	1,064.443	50.901	37.644	320.878	1,000.000	1,409.423

See Appendix Tables A–G.

Note: In this table, SE means earnings from currency issue, BT means tax contributions of state-owned banks, FS is the financial support of state-owned banks, MC is the management cost of state-owned banks, SC is the supervision cost of the central bank, SI is the savings interest of state-owned banks and BD is the bad debts of state-owned banks.

Table 2.6 The return-cost index of financial control by the state: 1979–1996

(Billion Yuan)

Year	IR_m				IC_m					P^i
	IR^g_m	ISE	IBT	IFS	IC^g_m	IMC	ISC	ISI	IBD	
1979	0.100	10.000	10.000	10.000	0.100	10.000	10.000	10.000	10.000	10.000
1980	0.158	13.562	3.073	20.953	0.220	12.153	10.000	19.380	27.994	10.600
1981	0.123	8.942	3.528	17.678	0.129	17.639	10.000	25.409	6.504	10.854
1982	0.149	7.709	3.888	18.367	0.228	23.727	10.000	34.951	15.789	11.061
1983	0.176	16.363	41.659	18.287	0.197	26.991	10.000	46.190	6.910	11.227
1984	0.396	46.724	187.463	22.204	0.222	41.157	10.000	62.866	0.722	11.541
1985	0.951	194.882	407.707	25.947	0.327	47.940	10.000	99.721	4.573	12.557
1986	0.716	81.194	489.659	40.695	0.562	84.630	16.803	144.753	32.102	13.310
1987	0.788	51.198	554.748	79.834	1.714	118.866	21.371	198.814	302.276	14.282
1988	0.883	132.895	546.829	95.823	1.966	162.778	33.328	295.103	394.737	16.924
1989	0.707	130.575	314.732	119.676	2.519	177.130	39.022	524.403	554.765	19.936
1990	1.118	242.122	634.390	153.078	2.682	187.778	45.328	546.047	618.777	20.355
1991	1.041	249.138	470.260	158.086	2.873	228.958	57.642	627.727	662.162	20.945
1992	1.008	238.017	403.707	183.603	4.031	306.690	77.170	798.652	1,066.856	22.076
1993	1.486	452.939	589.593	285.296	7.310	387.546	114.672	1,499.856	2,311.522	24.990
1994	1.065	511.584	220.797	223.392	7.137	745.579	204.533	2,122.875	2,489.331	30.413
1995	0.972	393.988	502.601	279.133	7.630	964.028	246.585	2,926.253	2,844.950	34.914
1996	1.738	1,135.634	609.805	341.910	8.253	1,178.264	328.769	2,883.010	3,556.188	37.044

Data source and note: The data in this table is calculated based on Table 2.5 of this book. The comprehensive index of return IR^g_m and the comprehensive index of cost IC^g_m of financial control by the state are acquired by weighting upon their respective subindices. All indices exclude the influence of the changes to prices P^i. The weighting coefficients of all indices are confirmed based on the proportion of the factor in the return or cost of financial control by the state (see Table H of Appendix), which are respectively estimated to be ISE 0.35, IBT 0.09, IFS 0.56, IMC 0.07, ISC 0.03, ISI 0.35 and IBD 0.55. The computation formulas are respectively $IR^g_m = (0.35 \text{ ISE} + 0.09 \text{ IBT} + 0.56 \text{ IFS}) M_{ti}$, and $IC^g_m = (0.07 \text{ IMC} + 0.03 \text{ ISC} + 0.35 \text{ ISI} + 0.55 \text{ IBD}) M_{ti}$. M_{ti} refers to the monetization level and indicates the year in this table.

use the estimate value or approximate alternative value for any data that cannot be accurately acquired. Therefore, the data in the table could suggest the trend of changes of the return and cost of financial control by the state but should better not be applied as the reference data.

Seen from Table 2.5, the gross return exceeded the gross cost of financial control by the state from 1979 to 1991. The net earning acquired by the state amounted to 693.959 billion Yuan. This was the exact reason for the state to rapidly expand the monopoly financial property rights and take the initiative to strengthen financial control at the beginning of the reform. Nevertheless, the cost quickly exceeded the return of financial control by the state after 1992. The net cost paid by the state reached as high as 1,657.092 billion Yuan between 1992 and 1996. As a result, the state started applying passive financial control instead of the previous active control. Then, why do we regard the year 1988 as the turning point for the active financial control by the state to become passive since the cost of financial control by the state exceeded the return in 1992? To answer this question, it is necessary to investigate the trend of changes of the return and cost indices of financial control by the state. According to Table 2.6 and Figure 2.3, the cost index curve of financial control by the state was relatively as flat as the return index curve before 1986. For example, if the return index and the cost index were 1.0 in 1979, the cost index and the return index in 1986 were respectively 5.62 and 7.16. After 1986, the curve of the return index was still flat, while the curve of the cost index suddenly became steep. For instance, the cost index rapidly grew to 17.14 in 1987, 9.26 higher than

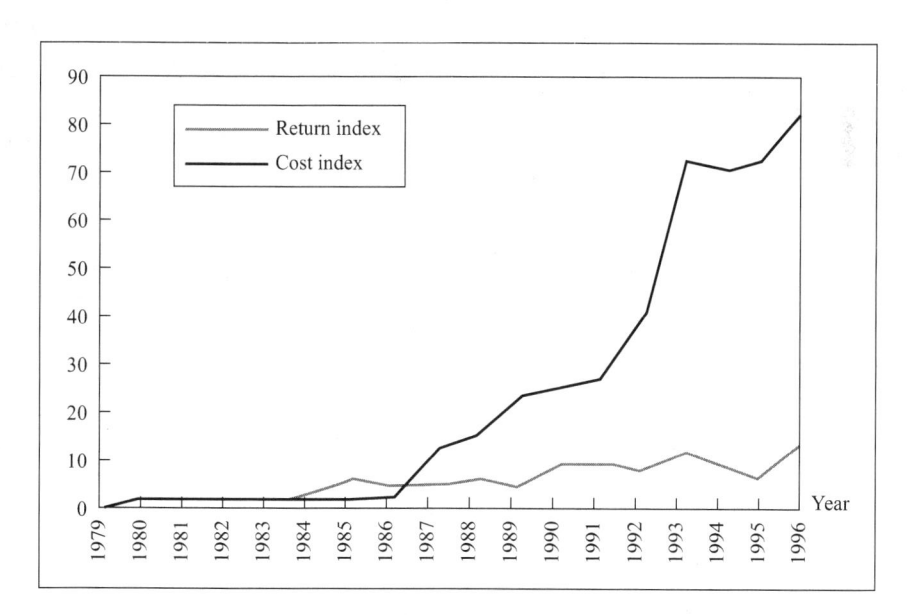

Figure 2.3 Trend of changes to the return-cost index of financial control by the state

Data source: Table 2.6 of this book.

the return index. After that, the distance between the curve of the cost index and the curve of the return index became increasingly greater, reaching a difference of 65.15 by 1996. Although the cost of financial control by the state only surpassed the return by 1992 in terms of the absolute value, the state had been exposed to the huge pressure of rapid growth of the cost of financial control (compared to the small changes to the return from the control) since 1986 in terms of the utility function of financial control by the state. Since then, the state had no strong internal incentive to control finance as it had done at the early stage of the reform. Moreover, although the return from financial control was still increasing and the state was still able to make profits, financial control has become more difficult. The state became more cautious in financial control particularly after the financial setback in 1988.

Notes

1 These proportions were all calculated by professor Ronald Mckinno and disagree with the data listed in Table 2.2 of this book. The values in parentheses are added by the author.
2 Why was China able to maintain rapid growth when conducting partial and phased reform, but why did CEE (Central and Eastern Europe countries of centrally planned economy) and NIS (Newly Independent States of CIS) encounter significant decline in their bolder reforms? The World Bank (1996a) believed that favorable initial conditions of China constituted the first step in solving the mystery (page 19).
3 This calculation results of the World Bank also disagree with the corresponding data in Table 2.2 of this book.

3 Financial support to the gradual reform

The success of the gradual reform in China has always drawn wide attention from domestic and foreign economists. In general, people are interested in the same question of why China, different from the Soviet Union and Eastern Europe of the same system, embarked on the road of gradual reform, or what factors contributed to the success of the gradual reform in China. Sheng Hong (1996) and Zhang Jun (1997a) have given great explanations to this question, so the general question about the gradual reform will not be discussed in this chapter. In view of the topic of this book, we are more interested in what role financial factors are playing in the gradual reform. In this chapter, we demonstrate that financial factors are playing the special supporting role or even the key role in the gradual reform of China. Without understanding the financial factors, it is impossible to comprehensively and accurately describe and explain the road of gradual reform in China.

1 Growth during the transition and financial factors

I Existing discussions: what people missed

Domestic and foreign economists hold different opinions on the economic growth during the transition in China compared to the failure of the Soviet Union and Eastern Europe due to different focuses and perspectives. There are generally two explanations, initial conditions and the way of reform. Then what indeed contributed to the success of gradual reform in China, the advantages of the initial conditions or the good choice of the way of reform? When economists emphasize the comparative advantages of the initial conditions, they put too much emphasis on a static situation or the situation at a certain time at the beginning of the reform. For example, when the reform began, the Chinese economy was exposed to a low industrialization level, and 71% of labor forces were absorbed by agriculture, compared to over 40% of labor forces in the industry sector in the Soviet Union; social security in China only covered employees of state-owned sectors, accounting for merely 20% of the total population, while social security in the Soviet Union covered nearly all people. It suggests the backwardness advantage of China. Moreover, when the reform began, the degree of central planning and level of central control in the Chinese economy were far lower than those of the Soviet

Union. In the 1970s, the central government of the Soviet Union distributed about 60,000 kinds of commodities through planning, compared to only 600 in China in 1978. Even at the peak of the planned economy in China, there were still about 30,000 active markets in rural area. In view of this, China enjoyed enough space for rapid economic growth during the partial and phased reform. According to statistics, the GDP of the Soviet Union and Eastern Europe (including Mongolia) decreased by 6.8% each year on average between 1986 and 1995, while the GDP of China saw annual growth by 9.4% from 1978 to 1995. In this way, it was unnecessary for China to break the original structure for distribution of resource stocks, and radical reform based on stock adjustment was avoided. The increments of resources were allocated to non-state-owned sectors that were restricted in the traditional system (World Bank, 1997, page 16; World Bank, 1996a, pages 18–20; Fan Gang, 1996, pages 158–163; Lin Yifu et al., 1994). For the planned economy incorporating a huge agricultural sector, economic reform is like normal economic development, as it is a process of industrialization where labor forces transfer from the agricultural sector of low productivity to the industry sector of higher productivity. However, in the Soviet Union and Eastern Europe, urbanization and industrialization had been completed, so their core issue was structural adjustment, that is, decreasing employment in the industry sector of low efficiency that enjoyed subsidies and increasing new employment opportunities in the industry and service sector of higher efficiency. By comparison, normal economic development is always easier than structural adjustments (Sachs & Woo, 1994a, 1994b). Nevertheless, few economists mentioned the essential condition, the different monetization levels, when emphasizing the importance of initial conditions.[1] In the light of the detailed discussion in Chapter 2 of this book, the difference in the monetization level actually exerted key influence on the process and results of reform, particularly economic growth during the transition. Considering the sharp decline of the state treasury in the reform and gains from monetization, certain close logical connections between initial conditions and the way of reform can be seen.

Maybe because the difference in the monetization level is not considered when initial conditions are emphasized, the financial factor has been ignored in economists' researches. But as a matter of fact, the contributions of the financial factor to economic growth are becoming increasingly prominent along with the treasury support-oriented economy transforming to a financial support-oriented economy during the reform. It is evidently inappropriate to discuss the reform and growth in transition when ignoring the financial factor (or placing it in the secondary position). This is the point where the idea on the way of reform conflicts with the idea about initial conditions. Since both have neglected monetization or the financial factor, the two, originally of internal logical connection, are considered incompatible. However, if the financial factor is introduced, the difference in the way of reform (the gradual and radical reform) can be exactly attributed to the differences in initial conditions.

The idea about the way of reform has proposed many explanations on the economic growth of China during transition. The way of reform can be generally divided into "out-system" (or out-plan) growth and "in-system" (or in-plan) growth. At the same time, both can be contained under the concept of "dual-track gradual growth". However, the variable of the financial factor has been neglected in all these ideas, or, in other words, the financial factor has not been regarded as the major variable or has been completely neglected in the hypothesis in the model of theoretical analysis. For example, Naughton (1994) believed that the reform strategies applied by China constituted the important factor or major variable for the success of reform, while the dual-track system enabled the out-system growth of the economy after the reform of China. This was because the previous state monopoly was relaxed in the reform and therefore emerging sectors joined the market. The state-owned sector had to improve itself due to the competition. In this way, the dual-track system realized such a "virtuous cycle" of reform in China. According to Fan Gang (1994), the key of the gradual reform in China lay in developing the new system outside the old system, instead of changing the state-owned system in the first place, and relying on the growth of the non-state-owned economy to support the stable transition of the system. Anyhow, the theory on out-system growth and the theory on out-system reform both prefer the contributions of out-system sectors to economic growth during the transition. However, how was the in-system or in-system growth sustained, and how was the rapid decline avoided, in addition to the out-system growth and out-system reform? The theory on out-system reform fails to give enough attention to in-system reform, maybe because the out-system reform theory of China only focuses on the growth of out-system sectors. But based on discussions in Chapter 2, financial support does not make an important part in out-system growth, so it was unnecessary to incorporate the financial factor in researches. This may be the reason why the financial factor is ignored in the out-system reform theory.

Zhang Jun (1997a) attempted to explain the significance of the gradual reform based on in-system growth. He thought that the existence and growth of the out-system or out-system sector could explain the success of China indeed but failed to reveal the experiences in the Soviet Union. As the Soviet Union had set up the out-system departments between 1985 and 1989, no out-system growth had been achieved. Therefore, he directed his eyes to the state-owned system and the in-system growth, that is, how to sustain the in-system growth or production of state-owned sectors in the dual-track reform. The success of the dual-track system in China could be attributed to the dual-track price system under restrictions of quotas in China (the Soviet Union failed in the dual-track system since it had no dual-track price system). One foundation contributing to the out-system success lay in the stable in-system transition at the early stage of the reform. Without the stable in-system transition, the out-system economy would be necessarily exposed to L-shaped growth during transition as merely relying on the in-system "supply loss". A powerful centralized government was needed to ensure compulsory execution of planned quotas of state-owned sectors, thus to sustain the stable development of production of traditional state-owned sectors during the transition. Due to restrictions of quotas, the non-state-owned sector could only acquire out-system outputs or inputs with market prices and would be unlikely to develop by stealing resources from the state-owned sector (page 206). Zhang Jun was accurate in explaining the government capacity and restrictions of quotas. This point is also regarded as the key variable to realization of financial support in later discussions. Anyhow, the theory of quota restriction is directly developed by Zhang Jun from the theory of "inputs loss" of Murphy, which has covered the shortage of the theory on out-system growth and shown the significant value. Murphy, Shleifer, and Vishny (1992) originally believed that the financial factor would be introduced as the theory started concerning the in-system issue. However, Zhang Jun failed to give due consideration to the financial factor in the "revised model of the leading sector" created by him (page 247). Although he mentioned that state-owned enterprises continued enjoying the right to acquire the cheap credit provided by government banks while emphasizing the subsidies, this point was not reflected by this model. It should not be ignored considering the importance of financial subsidies to the stable in-system transition. Although it should not be considered a defect, it undermined the explanatory power of the model.

The model of the quota restriction theory has, to a great extent, explained why the state-owned industry sector could sustain the growth of production during the transition period, but a series of questions may arise after further thinking about how the growth was sustained. If the answer is relying on subsidies, then how could subsidies be sustained against the rapid reduction of the treasury? Moreover, what about the corresponding cost of the in-system growth that helped the stable transition of the system? As a matter of fact, the economic reform threw a heavy burden on the financial sector along with the stable in-system growth. The quota restriction only transferred but did not break down or relieve the risks and costs of the reform. Then, should it be considered a successful reform from the perspective of the overall reform process (the theory of quota restriction is only concerned about the reform and growth of the state-owned industry sector)? The final conclusion on the success of the overall reform should only be drawn after certain results of the financial reform.

On this basis, initial conditions cannot be ignored by those holding the theory of the way of reform. It shall be noted that the initial conditions here incorporated the initial condition of the financial factor, so initial conditions are important once the financial factor is introduced. Actually, if attention is given to the whole economy during the transition instead of only the state-owned economic sector, the significance of initial conditions became prominent immediately. Therefore, the analysis of partial equilibrium shall be extended to the analysis of general equilibrium, as emphasized in the Introduction of this book. A model of in-system growth incorporating the financial factor shall be developed. For the micro-model of in-system growth, initial conditions shall be regarded as the exogenous variable for the convenience of discussions. As also believed by Zhang Jun (1997a), the differences in initial conditions are apparently the exogenous factor for the economic reform, while the exogenous factor will not become the decisive factor that affects the results of reform, although it will interact with some internal factors (page 308). Importantly, it is still essential to endogenize some exogenous factors. Once some exogenous factors are transformed to be endogenous factors, the results of the analysis would be changed and would better fit practical conditions. For an example, Ronald Coase and Douglass North only triggered an unprecedented revolution of economics after endogenizing the transaction costs and institutions that were regarded as the exogenous factor by the neoclassical framework. It suggests that the development of economics is essentially the constant process of endogenizing exogenous factors. For an economic institution under reform, the most profound issue is often hidden behind some exogenous variables.

Now let's discuss why initial conditions become important once the financial factor is introduced. As pointed out earlier, the quota restriction by the government laid the foundation to sustain in-system growth during the reform, among which the credits are occupying an increasing proportion. For example, the average debt ratio of state-owned enterprises (within the system) is approximately 80%, and reaches over 90% in 80% of these enterprises, and from the late 1980s to the early 1990s, the net funds flow to state-owned enterprises from banks accounted for 7% to 8% of GDP (Zhang Jie, 1997a). According to Xiao Geng's research (1995), the proportion of the budgetary fund in the production and investment fund newly injected each year dropped from 92.3% in 1972 to 24.2% in 1991, while the decline of the liquid capital among the fund was more evident, for instance, from 57.5% in 1972 to 0.6% in 1991. At the same time, the proportion of state-owned banks in the newly invested funds increased from 7.7% to 75.8%, where their proportion in the liquid capital rose from 42.5% to 99.4%. According to our calculation, state-owned banks took up 84.6% of the production and investment funds newly injected in 1996, and the liquid capital accounted for 99.3%. Please see more details in Table 3.1. It can be seen that without the great financial support, the in-system growth and the stable transition of the system would be a dream.

Then, where does the big sum of financial resources come from, and how are they allocated to state-owned enterprises? As discussed in Chapter 2, a great amount of gains from monetization, including financial surpluses in particular (mainly household saving deposits), have been acquired along with the reform due to the monetization interval. Meanwhile, the state is able to control and allocate these surpluses. The monetization interval and control of the state constituted the special initial conditions for the reform in China compared to the Soviet Union and Eastern Europe, and these factors enabled the growth of the state-owned sector at the early stage of the reform and the success of the dual-track transition (gradualism). Why the state was able to apply the quota restriction was first because the state enjoyed the conditions for application of the restriction, particularly the financial conditions. Without these conditions, the state would find no way to adopt the restriction even though it wanted to (since the restriction complies with its goal of the maximum rent). It was difficult to implement the gradual reform in the Soviet Union because the initial conditions or exogenous condition such as financial surpluses were lacking (especially the rapid reduction of household deposits) and state control was weakened, but not because there was any error in the reform method (i.e., the quota restriction was not applied) or people were not willing to apply or accept the way. In case of the rapid decline of fiscal capacity (the common situation in China, the Soviet Union and Eastern Europe), the great amount of financial surpluses and the strong state capacity were needed to maintain the quota

Table 3.1 Changes of proportions of treasury and finance in capital for production and investment of state-owned economies in China: 1972–1996

	Fiscal funds from the government (billion Yuan)			Loans from state-owned banks (billion Yuan)			Increase of loans from state-owned banks (billion Yuan)			Total (%) (1)/[(1)+(7)]	Fixed capital (%) (2)/[(2)+(8)]	Liquid capital (%) (3)/[(3)+(9)]
	Total	Fixed capital	Liquid capital	Total	Fixed capital	Liquid capital	Total	Fixed capital	Liquid capital			
	(1)	(2)	(3)	(4)	(5)	(6)	(7)	(8)	(9)	(10)	(11)	(12)
1972	37.750	33.455	4.295	114.560		114.560	3.170		3.170	92.3	100.0	57.5
1973	39.648	34.266	5.382	126.900		126.900	12.340		12.340	76.3	100.0	30.4
1974	38.479	34.003	4.476	135.350		135.350	8.450		8.450	82.0	100.0	34.6
1975	40.027	35.843	4.184	146.270		146.270	10.920		10.920	78.6	100.0	27.7
1976	39.095	34.559	4.536	154.180		154.180	7.910		7.910	83.2	100.0	36.4
1977	40.601	34.033	6.568	166.330		166.330	12.150		12.150	77.0	100.0	35.1
1978	58.176	51.516	6.660	185.000		185.000	18.670		18.670	75.7	100.0	26.3
1979	63.877	58.671	5.206	203.960	0.790	203.170	18.960	0.790	18.170	77.1	98.7	22.3
1980	53.655	49.984	3.671	241.430	5.550	235.880	37.530	4.760	32.770	58.9	91.3	10.1
1981	41.877	39.593	2.284	286.020	8.340	277.680	44.590	2.790	41.800	48.4	93.4	5.2
1982	40.180	37.817	2.363	318.060	23.810	294.250	32.040	15.470	16.570	55.6	71.0	12.5
1983	47.441	46.152	1.289	358.990	30.710	328.280	40.930	6.900	34.030	53.7	87.0	3.6
1984	61.066	60.070	0.996	476.610	45.170	431.440	117.620	14.460	103.160	34.2	80.6	1.0
1985	70.152	68.722	1.430	590.560	70.530	520.030	113.950	25.360	88.590	38.1	73.0	1.6
1986	81.161	80.167	0.994	759.080	100.590	658.490	168.520	30.060	138.460	32.5	72.7	0.7
1987	76.511	75.305	1.206	903.250	128.680	774.570	144.170	28.090	116.080	34.7	72.8	1.0
1988	79.397	78.438	0.959	1,055.130	155.923	899.207	151.880	27.243	124.637	34.3	74.2	0.8
1989	78.415	77.206	1.209	1,240.930	177.596	1,063.334	185.800	21.673	164.127	29.7	78.1	0.7
1990	89.041	87.951	1.090	1,511.640	224.575	1,287.065	270.710	46.979	223.731	24.8	65.2	0.5

1991	93.364	92.056	1.308	1,804.395	304.436	1,499.959	292.755	79.861	212.894	24.2	53.5	0.6
1992	99.906	98.843	1.063	2,161.550	392.460	1,769.090	357.155	88.024	269.131	21.9	52.9	0.4
1993	134.069	132.221	1.848	2,646.110	517.050	2,129.060	484.560	124.590	359.970	21.7	51.5	0.5
1994	107.218	105.485	1.733	3,244.130	801.130	2,443.000	598.020	284.080	313.940	15.2	27.1	0.5
1995	131.280	127.780	3.500	3,939.360	1,002.560	2,936.800	695.230	201.430	493.800	15.9	38.8	0.7
1996	145.900	141.600	4.300	4,743.470	1,203.420	3,540.050	804.110	200.860	603.250	15.4	41.3	0.7

Data source: Table 16.2 of Xiao Geng (1997), Table F.7 of the *Report on China's National Conditions: 1978–1995*, Table 3.7 of *China Financial Outlook* (1997) and Table 22 of the World Bank (1997).

restriction. In other words, the execution of quota restriction was not free but demanded a huge cost. The primary and practical issue lay in whether the state could afford the implementation of quota restriction and whether the efficient mechanism to pay the cost existed, and then the question would be how to perform the quota restriction. Therefore, as the more reasonable explanation, the special initial conditions in China decided the success of the dual-track transition. Apparently, certain logical connection could be found between initial conditions and the way of reform. Initial conditions constituted the necessary condition for the success of dual-track gradual reform in China (not in the Soviet Union), while the way of reform made up the condition for realization of growth during the transition. Both were indispensable. It would be unrealistic to choose the way of reform for an economy free from any restriction of the subjective or objective condition and carry out the reform in a closed neoclassical framework. The World Bank (1996a) correctly pointed out that differences in initial conditions and institutional features might be the reason for different results and policies of transitions in different countries. The correct portfolio proposal of reform must reflect initial conditions but shall not be purely transplanted from one country to another country, like between the Soviet Union and China (page 21). In other words, the different performances of transitions in the Soviet Union, Eastern Europe and China did not result from the choice of the way of reform, but were derived from something that could not be transplanted. Without any doubt, the initial conditions (i.e., the institutional factors) were the most difficult to transplant. For an instance, the orange tree cannot be transplanted to the north from the south, not because of any problem with the orange tree but due to differences in initial conditions between the north and south (such as the climate and soil).

II   *The difference in savings and performance of the transition*

It can be seen from these preliminary discussions that the financial factor must be considered for accurate and comprehensive understanding of the success of the reform in China (or the path of the gradual reform). Nevertheless, the financial factor is not simple but is full of complexity. The savings issue is first discussed here.

As a matter of fact, according to existing studies, attention had once been given to the role of the financial factor in the gradual reform in China. As mentioned prior, a development report of the World Bank (1996a) had once considered the financial factor as an important initial condition for the success of reform in China. This report believed that the development of financial systems in China and Russia showed great differences at the beginning of the transition. The financial system of China was underdeveloped, and the monetary stock (M2) only equaled 25% of GDP, but the economy in Russia had already been monetized by 1990. As pointed out in Chapter 2, under these circumstances, monetization, growth of household deposits, institutional changes and economic growth could be propelled simultaneously in China. However, the high monetization level at the beginning of the reform in Russia not only implied that the great amount of monetary accumulation accrued by compulsory savings had become the fund support by the government to the planned economy, but also indicated that the release of the price control and fiscal monetization would necessarily lead to extremely severe inflation, people's monetary accumulation (savings certificates) of no value and finally the sharp decline of the monetary stock and breakdown of the financial system of the state. As shown in Figure 3.1, the domestic savings rate of China was quite similar to the rate of the Soviet Union and Eastern European countries at the beginning of the reform (approximately 35%). Right after the beginning of the reform, the savings rate of later countries had dropped significantly, while the savings rate of China had maintained a high level. It can be seen that the savings rate (particularly the household deposits rate) constituted a key to understanding of the success of

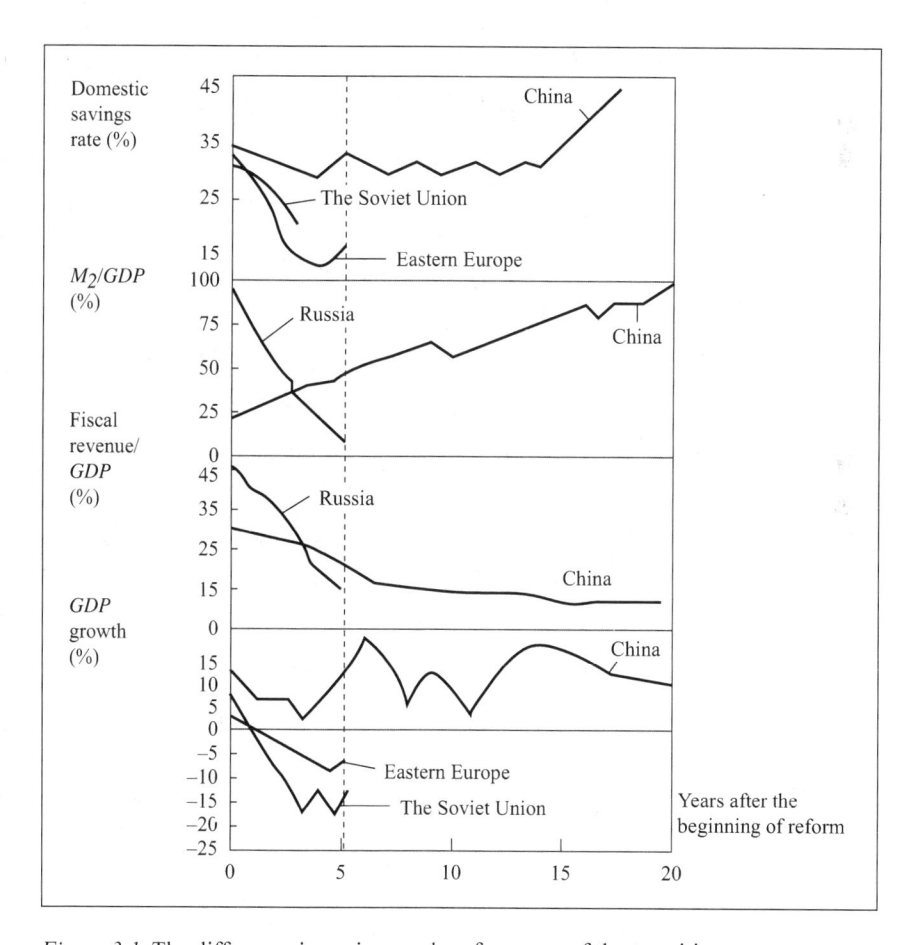

Figure 3.1 The difference in savings and performance of the transition

Data source: Table 1.2, Figure 2.3 and Figure 2.5 of World Bank (1996a) and Figure 1.4 of World Bank (1997) and Chapter 2 of this book.

gradual reform in China. Also according to Figure 3.1, the proportion of fiscal revenue in GDP dropped both in China and Russia (representing the Soviet Union and Eastern Europe) and was even lower in China. At the same time, China had maintained rapid growth of GDP, while the GDP in the Soviet Union and Eastern European countries was exposed to J-shaped or L-shaped decline. The key to the situation was that the domestic savings rate and M2/GNP of China had steadily developed since the reform, in contrast to the Soviet Union and Eastern European countries. To sum up, the gradual reform in China benefited from the relative financial stability. During the reform, China had applied complete and prudent monetary policies including household deposits and treasury bonds. In particular, China adopted household deposits to cover deficits of enterprises during the transition and, in this way, avoided severe financial instability and vigorously supported in-system growth. Although the government rendered subsidies and increased low-interest loans to non-profit state-owned enterprises at the cost of low efficiency, China can stand the cost by now without fundamental influence on the economy because of the great amount of household deposits (World Bank, 1997, page 25).

III   Significance of state capacity

Savings only constitute a part of the financial factor that supports the gradual transition of the economy. Moreover, the high household deposits rate is conditional. We noticed that state capacity was another key to this issue.

In addition to the cause of savings, the different performances of economic transitions in China, the Soviet Union and Eastern Europe also resulted from the great difference in the state capacity in economic control, as shown in Figure 3.2. Based on Chapter 2, despite the rapid decline of fiscal capacity since the reform, state capacity has been reflected and sustained through "strong finance".

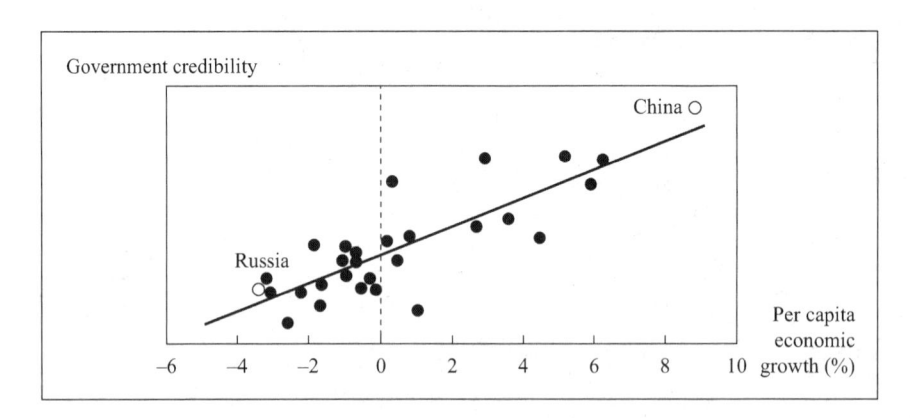

Figure 3.2 Government credibility and its effect on economic growth

Data source: The data of foreign countries is introduced from Figure 5.1 of World Bank (1996a), and the data of China is estimated by the author.

Apparently, the high savings rate was a necessary condition instead of a sufficient condition to growth during the transition in China. The sufficient condition should have been a strong government that could centralize the savings in a certain form as the financial support to economic outputs (particularly the in-system outputs). Ronald Mckinnon has proposed many influential opinions on financial issues during the transition since the 1990s. When commenting on the reason why China and Eastern Europe (including the Soviet Union) led a different way of reform, he pointed out that explanations of the decline of outputs in Eastern Europe should consider its exterior political and economic environment where outputs were mostly free from economic control by a single government under reform, which was completely different than China. In addition to the level of industrialization and trade impact, the power of communist parties in most Eastern European countries and the Soviet Union had been greatly reduced during the reform. Therefore, the centralized political control by the state over the whole economy and the decentralized supervision by the Party on state-owned enterprises had been severely weakened. It is because China has always kept powerful government control during the reform that the state could overcome restrictions of the taxation system despite the rapid decline of fiscal capacity and make use of the state-owned banking system to rapidly centralize savings that are scattered among the people and have increased along with the progress of monetization. In this way, the state was still able to control the marginal price of state-owned enterprises exposed to traditional soft budgetary restraints and provide great fund support despite the weak treasury. Powerful control by the state also created the necessary condition for the formation and collection of savings. Holders of savings certificates of state-owned banks have no misgiving on risks based on the reliable reputation of the state, since the state rendered an implied guarantee for savings of the state-owned banking system (World Bank, 1997, page 10).[2] Meanwhile, the state had kept a positive practical interest rate in most years, so the cash currencies held by residents and the yield rate of savings certificates were stable although not very high. According to the research of Ronald Mckinnon (1996), the policies of China on the interest rate, especially the interest rate of savings, had played a significant role in stimulating residents and enterprises to accumulate their financial assets. If the index of retail prices in China is applied as the criterion for annual inflation, the Chinese government has done a very good job in retaining the positive savings interest rate. In particular, against the high inflation rate between 1988 and 1989, the government was able to rapidly respond to the situation and performed full indexation of some interest rates, such as raising the nominal interest rate of three-year household fixed deposits by 20% to 26% in this period and thus maintaining the positive value of the practical interest rate. The huge amount of increase of financial assets stock arising this way enabled the financing by liberalized sectors for these sectors themselves as well as the deficits of the government and state-owned enterprises under slow reform (pages 263–264 and 283). The World Bank (1996a) believed that the original economic structure and powerful macroeconomic control in China had transformed the growth proceeds from local liberalization to a great amount of savings and financial assets of families. It acted as a cushion to the adverse effect of the state-owned sector that was still an economic burden by 1996 and guaranteed the process of reform (page 22).

We can imagine that without adequate control capacity of the state, regional forces and state-owned banks owning "private benefits" would act as they pleased due to marketization and decentralization and would make use of their right of credit control gradually acquired to apply credit funds to any place that fit their own interests more (mainly the non-state-owned sector). Then, the supply of financial resources to the state-owned sector would be insufficient and the in-system outputs would drop. However, in China, no matter how strongly local governments and state-owned banks requested "private benefits" and how they tried to escape from control, they failed to fundamentally shake the dominant role of the state in controlling financial resources. As pointed out in Chapter 2, the state had successfully made 35% of loans of the major four specialized banks as the policy-related loan and effectively restricted the interest pursuit of state-owned banks that were inconsistent with the state preference. Moreover, the state also carried out strict control over the credit scale and the corresponding high reserves system, and the legal deposit reserve ratio (including the provision ratio) had once achieved 18% to 24%. In this way, the state had greatly restricted the capability of state-owned banks to independently apply credit funds and thus used the majority of the funds to support the quota restriction (i.e., using the credit quota to support the outputs quota) and in-system growth. Now we can easily understand why the marketization level of the banking sector was far lower than all other non-financial sectors. State-owned banks were serving the administrative leadership rather than industrial enterprises. Although central planning played an increasingly smaller role in all other sectors during the reform, administrative control of the central government over state-owned banks was strengthening (Qian Yingyi, 1995, Page 142).

As clearly shown in Figure 3.3, the government capacity in China presented an evident positive correlation to the monopoly level of state-owned finance, low inflation rate and GDP growth. It was completely different in the Soviet Union and Eastern Europe. With the Soviet Union as an example, although the financial deficit increased between 1988 and 1990 and control over the prices of most industrial products was not relieved, the function of the banking industry in the whole economy of the Soviet Union had been exposed to decentralization rapidly, which could lead to money out of control in a larger scale. In 1988, the government started to break the monopoly by state-owned banks and established more specialized intermediary organizations to render credits to industry and agriculture. If these banks were still owned and governed by the state, the financial system would be centralized enough and the central bank would not lose control over credits. However, the state empowered all republics to jointly manage banks at their places in 1990. As a result, organs broadly known as commercial banks (wildcat banks) quickly increased from 1989 to 1990. The monopoly structure of state-owned finance had disappeared since the beginning of the reform (Ronald Mckinnon, 1996, pages 205–206).

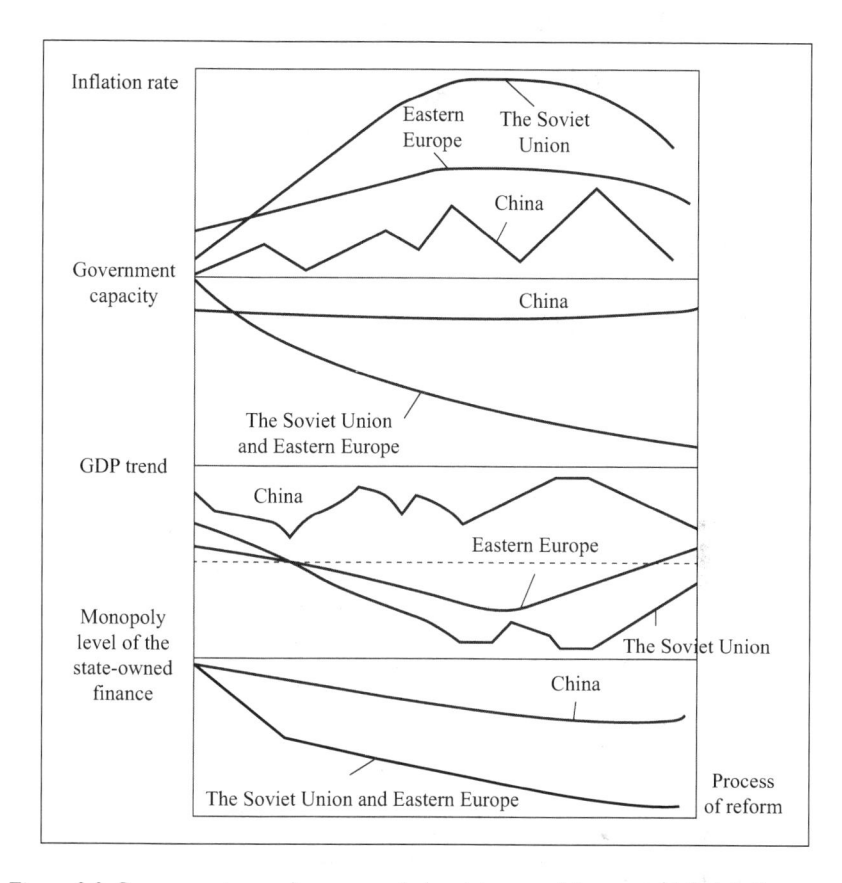

Figure 3.3 Government capacity, monopoly by state-owned finance and their influence

Gérard Roland (1995) once defined the strong government as the government possessing the right of schedule and defined the weak government as the prey of rent-seeking of lobbies and interest groups. According to him, although rent-seeking was commonly seen at all levels of the economy during the reform in China, the experiences in China could be better understood with the framework of the right of schedule. The rent-seeking framework in China might not have been as effective as the framework of the right of schedule, as the state always successfully kept relative control over the schedule in any case. By comparison, the sudden break-down of the central authority in Eastern Europe led to institutional vacuum, greatly expanding the set of possible political results. Therefore, the collisions and interest conflicts among pressure groups could result in paralysis of the decision-making system, so resources could not be allocated in an effective and centralized manner before the institutional structure was reorganized and production capacity was restored. Outputs rapidly declined in the end.

2   Financial subsidies and in-system growth

I   Fiscal subsidies and financial subsidies: an estimate

As mentioned, the successful transition of the Chinese economy mainly benefited from the stable growth of in-system outputs, while the control capacity of
the Chinese government (quota restriction) and the great amount of subsidies to
state-owned enterprises protected in-system outputs from recessions like in the
Soviet Union and Eastern European countries. The subsidies here mainly consisted of direct subsidies to deficits, price subsidies (for example, state-owned
enterprises could acquire some non-labor inputs from other state-owned enterprises at the planned prices lower than market prices) and institutional subsidies
(restriction on entry of other non-state-owned enterprises) and so on to state-
owned enterprises. According to Table 2.2 of this book, all kinds of subsidies
(open subsidies) to state-owned enterprises through fiscal budgets between 1985
and 1994 equaled approximately 5.63% of GDP on average. Nevertheless, fiscal
subsidies dropped each year during this period, from 7.5% of GDP in 1985 to
2.2% in 1994. At the same time, implicit subsidies (i.e., financial subsidies)
provided by state-owned financial channels were rising sharply. Generally speaking, fiscal subsidies made up the main part at the beginning of the reform, but
financial subsidies gradually took the dominant role as the reform was deepened,
as indicated in Figure 3.4.

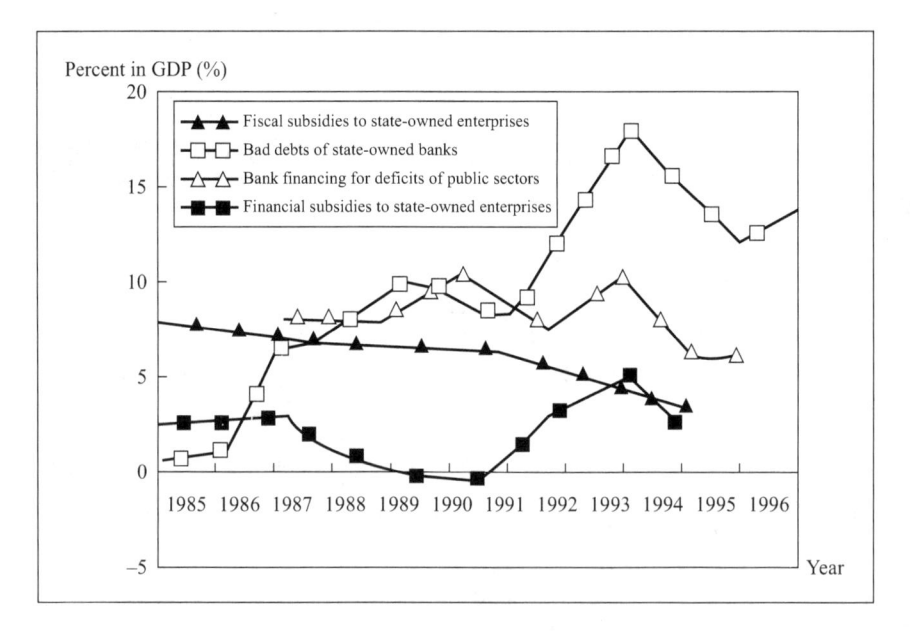

Figure 3.4 Fiscal subsidies and financial subsidies: trend since the reform

Data source: Table 2.2 and Table 2.5 of this book.

Table 3.2 Percentage of bad debts of state-owned banks in GDP

(%)											
1985	*1986*	*1987*	*1988*	*1989*	*1990*	*1991*	*1992*	*1993*	*1994*	*1995*	*1996*
0.14	0.74	7.11	7.44	9.22	9.36	8.61	11.26	18.81	15.06	13.88	14.75

Data source: This table is based on relevant data in Table 2.5 of this book.

Financial subsidies since the reform can be observed and studied from the following three aspects. First, according to statistics of the World Bank (see Table 2.2 of this book), financial subsidies, in the forms of low-interest-rate credits and unpaid principals, accounted for 1.72% of GDP on average between 1985 and 1994 and once reached as high as 3.6% in 1992. It shall be noted that the World Bank apparently underestimated the scale of financial subsidies. Second, the fiscal subsidies to state-owned enterprises already incorporated a part of financial contributions, since the state treasury directly gained great financial support from the state-owned finance. Also based on statistics of Table 2.2 of this book, the deficit of public sectors in China (including the government budget and state-owned enterprises) occupied 11.16% of GDP on average between 1987 and 1995, compared to 8.2% of financing from financial channels. According to Table 2.5 and Table C of the Appendix of this book, the financial support from state-owned banks to the state treasury had always been the major gains of financial control by the state, which accounted for 55.55% of total gains on average between 1979 and 1996 and amounted to 406.77 billion Yuan by 1996. A considerable part of the gains had been transformed to be fiscal subsidies to state-owned enterprises. Third, excessive debts of state-owned enterprises owed to state-owned banks and the large amount of bad debts were practically a kind of financial subsidy from the state to state-owned enterprises. If all bad debts of state-owned banks were considered as the financial subsidy, they occupied 9.7% of GDP on average from 1985 to 1996 and reached as high as 18.81% in 1993. See details in Table 3.2.

II   An in-system growth model considering financial subsidies

As mentioned in Section 1, Point 1 of this chapter, Zhang Jun (1997a) created a revised model of the leading sector, attempting to extend the theory of industrial organization under the dual-track price system and explain the success of gradual reform in China. He considered the "constant subsidies to state-owned sectors" in the model. Now, after further separating it into fiscal subsidies and financial subsidies, we establish a specialized in-system growth model by listing financial subsidies as an independent part, in order to analyze the special significance of the financial factor to the gradual reform. The other two factors listed in Zhang Jun's model (control over the pricing power and entry of non-state-owned sectors) also played an important part from the financial perspective. The significance of

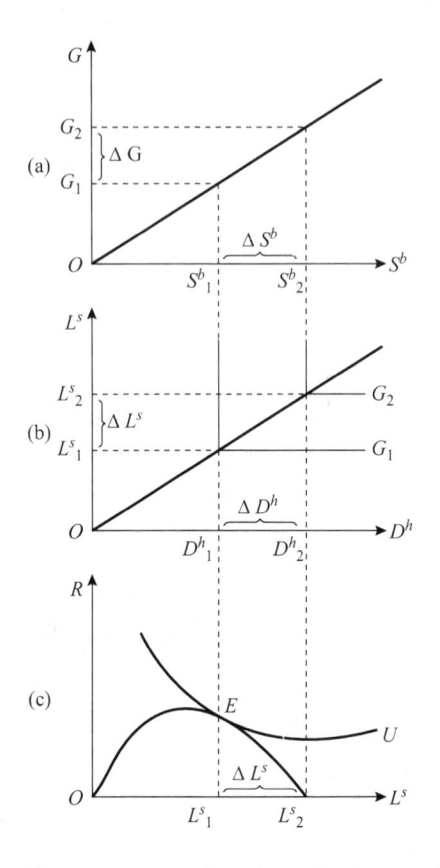

Figure 3.5 A function of in-system outputs based on a fixed proportion

control over the interest rate to the gradual reform will be mentioned in Chapter 4, and the entry of non-state-owned financial property right forms will be discussed in Chapter 5.

Figure 3.5 presents the model of the in-system growth considering financial subsidies. The following hypotheses are given for the convenience of the discussion. (1) During the reform, the state preferred to inhibit currency issue in order to prevent shaking people's confidence in the government under reform due to inflation and therefore always adopted prudent strategies on currency issue. This means that there was a strong government of risk aversion in the reform. On this basis, among many factors that support the growth of in-system outputs, the possibility that the government would apply more of the treasury to overdraft from banks or apply monetary expansion to render subsidies to state-owned enterprises and sustain the growth of outputs is ruled out. This matches the practical condition of gradual decrease of the proportion of fiscal subsidies. (2) The efficiency of in-system enterprises was commonly low. The hard fund gap had existed since the very beginning due to a severe shortage of capitals, so in-system enterprises were exposed to an extremely high debt ratio and greatly depended on state-owned banks. (3) The capital ratio of state-owned banks was also very low. Based on these three hypotheses, state-owned banks needed to sustain the supply of funds to in-system enterprises without monetary aid (investment) by the state (central bank), so they needed to collect a large amount of household deposits as the source of funds.

The growth of in-system outputs requires support by a certain amount of financial subsidies. Whether the deposits can grow in step with loans of state-owned banks decided the realization of financial subsidies. This means that we will see a production function with a nearly fixed proportion when considering the growth of in-system outputs. In other words, if the deposits (D^h) and loan provisions (L^s) are considered as two inputs to the growth of in-system outputs (G),[3] a specific combination of D^h and L^s shall be maintained to achieve a higher growth of outputs. The corresponding G can only be acquired by increasing D^h and L^s by the same proportion, as shown in Figure 3.5 (b). More strictly, both D^h and L^s are functions of the government capacity. Once the in-system production function is built on a fixed proportion, the choices of the state on the output modes will be limited. Or, the mode of financial subsidies generated within the system of China is not an option, but is decided by many endogenous and exogenous factors. We can further demonstrate the opinion we proposed that the choices of the way of reform (and the way of economic outputs) are conditional, and the initial conditions decide the way of reform and economic outputs.

It shall be noted that the economic outputs will be low if without adequate financial subsidies, as shown in Figure 3.5 (a). When the financial subsidy is relatively low at S^b_1, the economic growth will be G_1, and the low outputs of G_1 are insufficient to support the gradual institutional transition. To maintain a high level of outputs (such as G_2), corresponding inputs need to be added, such as increasing S^b, from S^b_1 to S^b_2, when D^h and L^s need to be respectively increased to D^h_2 and L^s_2 at the same time due to the fixed proportion of the production function. It is now necessary to reaffirm the following logical connection. To support the gradual reform, the in-system outputs shall be maintained at a higher level (G_2); against the rapid decline of the fiscal capacity, a great amount of financial subsidies (S^b_2) are needed to maintain the high G_2; since the state is a risk averter, a high L^s_2 is required to maintain a high S^b_2; but as the capitals owned by state-owned finance are also insufficient, the only choice is to do everything possible to maintain the mobilization capacity (the capacity of state-owned banks to attract deposits) of household deposits (financial surpluses) at the high level of D^h_2. It is fortunate that the specific monetization process in China lay the foundation for accumulation of household deposits.

The corresponding credit mechanism was demanded to effectively transform household deposits to financial subsidies. However, as indicated in Figure 3.5 (c), within a standard commercial banking system, the amount of credit provisions is decided by the point of contact E between the opportunity curve OEL^S_2 and the utility curve U. The optimum amount of credit provisions of commercial banks is

L^s_1 in this figure. If we assume that the amount of financial subsidies from state-owned banks matched the standard amount of credit provisions at the beginning of reform (or before government appropriations being replaced by loans), it means that $OL^S_1 = OS^b_1 = OD^h_1$. Apparently, the commercial banking system cannot match the state preference on maintaining the growth of in-system outputs. In other words, a state-owned banking system that operates based on government preference instead of commercial principles is demanded to maintain the high growth rate (G_2) of in-system outputs. For the state-owned banking system controlled by the government, the amount of credit provisions is free from the restriction of the point of contact E and can reach OL^s_2 to the maximum. In Figure 3.5 (c), we assume the corresponding deposits mobilization capacity and financial subsidies to be respectively OD^h_2 and OS^b_2, which jointly support the high growth of in-system outputs G_2. Therefore, the model for the growth of in-system outputs considering financial subsidies must incorporate a state-owned banking system. The delayed reform of the state-owned financial system is undoubtedly an endogenous variable in the logic of gradual reform.

A deduction can be further derived from these discussions that the too early commercialization of state-owned banks does not fit the logic of gradual reform. Once state-owned enterprises realize commercialized operation, the amount of credit provisions will be significantly reduced from OL^s_2 to OL^s_1. Then even if there is a huge amount of deposits, they cannot be transformed to be financial subsides to in-system outputs. State-owned banks exposed to commercialized operation will not attract so many deposits out of consideration of the marginal utility, so the final deposits and financial subsidies will be respectively reduced from OD^h_2 and OS^b_2 to the "standard" OD^h_1 and OS^b_1. If considering inflation after the state loses control over finance, the deposits of commercialized state-owned banks will be rapidly dropped below OD^h_1. As a result, the in-system growth in the transition will only reach the G_1 level (or even lower). It is more remarkable that if state-owned banks complete the system transformation before economic transition, they will become a financial organization pursuing maximum profits. Since no other financial property form can compete with them, state-owned banks will act as a monopolist, in other words, asking for higher prices of funds and providing less credit support. Then, the capital structure of state-owned enterprises which relies on credits from state-owned banks after reform (particularly government appropriations being replaced by loans) will collapse rapidly, leading to quick decline of outputs.[4] Nevertheless, state-owned banks had always been subject to control by the strong government during the reform of China, although the state had paid a great cost for the control (constraint) as pointed out in Chapter 2. On this basis, we conclude that the success of the gradual reform in China was achieved at the cost of delayed financial reform and accumulation of huge financial risks. From the perspective of the logic of the whole gradual reform, the payment of the cost exactly constituted the characteristics of the reform in China. Compared to the Soviet Union and Eastern European countries, China had already paid the cost during the reform. How much it cost had nothing to do with whether the cost could be afforded.

Notes

1 The annual report of the World Bank (1996a) once mentioned the difference in the monetization level at the beginning of reform between China and the Soviet Union (page 21). But based on materials known to the author, the opinion about the difference seemed to exert no influence or attract no attention in discussions on the path of reform in China.

2 I once pointed out in research (1997) that the state always bore an undertaking on risk relief for state-owned banks, so the critical point of the bad debts ratio of state-owned banks was decided by the maximum capacity of the government on fulfilling the undertaking of risk relief. As long as the government is powerful, the household deposits at state-owned banks will be stable.

3 Here we actually regard D^h and L^s as different inputs to one in-system manufacturer, though D^h and L^s are only two aspects of one financial variable. It is for the convenience of discussions here.

4 Many economists have had discussions on the performance of the state-owned sector in the transitional economy. They believed that when a huge state-owned sector was placed in a completely market-oriented environment, it would not improve allocation of resources, but would lead to a market structure of monopoly by the state-owned sector. The state-owned sector that occupied the majority of market shares and had no real hard budget constraint would necessarily prefer to control the emerging market, if without constraints by the central plan (Zhang Jun, 1997a, page 104).

4 The model of money demand during transition

The success achieved in the gradual reform of China under financial support has offered a challenge to the theory of financial deepening that was once popular. The neoclassical framework the theory of financial deepening relied on was incapable of explaining the economic growth and financial performance during transition. This chapter aims to build a model of money demand that can explain the conditions during the transition of China.

1 Neutrality of the interest rate

Many economists have shown interest in validating the model of financial deepening of Ronald Mckinnon and Edward Shaw (M-S model) since the model was proposed. As it should be, Ronald Mckinnon and Edward Shaw had made corresponding validations when putting forward the theoretical model, but they had never expected so many validations performed by others afterwards. According to Richard L. Kitchen (1986), 17 metrological validations were conducted in the decade from 1973 to 1984, including 13 validations justifying the model and only 4 suggesting falsification. In other words, the theory of financial deepening was able to explain the financial conditions of developing countries and guide their practices of financial reform.

The more authoritative validation was performed by IMF (1983) in a study on policies on the interest rate of developing countries led by A. Lanyi and R. Saracoglu. It demonstrated that practical financial growth showed a positive correlation with practical GDP growth and that the countries maintaining a positive practical interest rate enjoyed a higher practical financial growth rate. In this way, it proved the positive correlation between the practical interest rate of deposits and the practical GDP growth.[1] Alan Gelb (1989) analyzed the relationship between the average interest rate of deposits and practical GDP growth rate within three to six months in a comprehensive research for the World Bank. The result suggested that the average outputs growth was 5.6% in countries of positive practical interest rate, compared to 3.8% in countries of slightly negative practical interest rate and only 1.9% in countries of severely negative practical interest rate.[2] According to the "stiff" explanation (self-deprecating) made by Ronald Mckinnon (1996, pages 25–27) based on the two regression equations of Alan Gelb, by each rise of 1% of the practical interest rate of deposits, the outputs growth rate would increase by 0.2% to 0.25%. Among these validations of the model of financial deepening, the most famous one was the several comprehensive sequential transnational studies on Asian countries in the 1960s and 1970s made by M. Fry.[3] He reached a conclusion that "each rise of 1% of the practical interest rate of deposits towards the competitive market equilibrium level is associated with the increase of the economic growth rate by 0.5%" (1978, page 152).

However, these validation results did not apply to the situation in China. Although Ronald Mckinnon (1996) once emphasized that the Chinese government had done a very good job in maintaining the positive practical interest rate of deposits (page 283), it was evident that China did not rely on manipulating the variable of the interest rate of deposits to mobilize savings and promote economic growth since the reform. The following discussion demonstrates that GDP growth, growth of financial assets and the interest rate of deposits have no clear correlativity in China. It is important to note that the government had successively lowered the nominal interest rate of deposits after 1995. For instance, the interest rate of a one-year deposit in 1995 was 10.98%, which was lowered to 7.47% in 1996, 5.67% in 1997 and further to 5.22% in March 1998, but the lower interest rate did not affect money demand and economic growth. The model for the theory of financial deepening exactly saw a counter example in the process of gradual reform in China.

On the basis of the model for the theory of financial deepening, the lower money yield would result in smaller money demand and less willingness in household deposits. However, the money yield basically played a neutral part against the money demand during the reform in China, and the $\partial L/\partial (d-p^*) > 0$ in the model for the theory of financial deepening did not work. Theoretically, the money yield only exerted influence over deposits when residents held the investment demand. When the process of monetization started in China, people's money demand was mainly the transaction demand, and the transaction demand was only associated with the growth of incomes. Only if the transaction demand reached a certain level would people have the demand on deposits and investment. Moreover, the investment demand only emerged based on the condition of the opportunity cost. The state applied policies to restrict the development of other financial instruments in order to gather more savings in state-owned banks. These policies had relieved people from the opportunity cost of holding cash, which equaled the vector V in Edward Shaw's model. Suppose people could only choose between holding deposit certificates and holding other non-monetary financial assets. If no opportunity cost was given, people would find no loss by holding cash (or deposit certificates) no matter how low the money yield was.[4] If D^h represents the bank deposits, then $D^h = F(Y, V, d-p^*)$. According to these conditions in China, $\partial F/\partial Y > 0$, and $\partial F/\partial V = \partial F/\partial (d-p^*) = 0$. In other words, the money demand in China apparently depended on the growth of residents' incomes and was nearly non-related to $d-p^*$ and V.

This hypothesis of the neutrality of the interest rate can be validated through the preliminary regression analysis. Based on Table 4.1, establishing the simple linear

Table 4.1 The practical interest rate of deposits, growth of deposits and economic growth of China: 1979–1996

	Inflation rate (p*)	Nominal interest rate of deposits (d)	d − p*	Growth rate of deposits (D^h)	Economic growth rate (G)
1979	2.0	3.96	1.96	33.43	7.6
1980	6.0	5.40	−0.60	42.17	7.8
1981	2.4	5.40	3.00	31.09	4.5
1982	1.9	5.76	3.86	28.97	8.7
1983	1.5	5.76	4.26	32.14	10.3
1984	2.8	5.76	2.96	36.10	14.7
1985	8.8	6.84	−1.96	33.58	13.5
1986	6.0	7.20	1.20	37.90	8.8
1987	7.3	7.20	−0.10	37.35	11.6
1988	18.5	8.64	−9.86	23.69	11.3
1989	17.8	11.34	−6.46	35.39	4.1
1990	2.1	8.64	6.54	36.67	3.8
1991	2.9	7.56	4.66	31.38	9.2
1992	5.4	7.56	2.16	27.23	14.2
1993	13.2	10.98	−2.22	29.30	13.5
1994	21.7	10.98	−10.72	41.54	12.6
1995	14.8	10.98	−3.82	37.84	10.2
1996	6.1	8.33	2.23	29.86	9.7

Data source: Table F of Appendix and Table 2.4 of this book.

regression for the economic growth rate and the growth rate of deposits against the practical interest rate of deposits provides the following result:

$$G^h = 33.63 − 0.105(d − p^*) \tag{4.1}$$
$$(28.256) \quad (−0.419)$$
$$R^2 = 0.0109, DW = 2.107$$

$$G = 9.75 − 0.16(d − p^*) \tag{4.2}$$
$$(12.27) \quad (−0.967)$$
$$R^2 = 0.0552, DW = 1.0005$$

Although the goodness of fit of these two regression equations is poor, the equation itself indicates that $d − p^*$ shows insignificant effect on D^h and G during the gradual reform in China.[5] In particular, the regression equation (4.1) exactly reflects the unique situation in China during the reform that deposits have been rising significantly along with gradual reduction of the interest rate (such as between 1996 and 1998). As further deducted from the regression equation (4.2), China lowered the interest rate of loans along with the interest rate of deposits in recent years in order to reduce the financing cost of state-owned enterprises. The lower interest rate of loans would lead to a lower financing cost of state-owned enterprises and thus enables the higher growth rate of in-system outputs. Combining relevant discussions in Chapter 3, it is easy to understand that the policy on the low interest rate has boosted economic growth during the gradual reform as an important part of financial support. Based on another model of Olivier Blanchard (Zhang Jun, 1997a), if state-owned enterprises could be free from price control and freely choose prices, the total outputs would decline. If control over the interest rate was relieved and the interest rate became high, the financial subsidies hardly could be maintained and the state-owned economy would be exposed rapidly to J-shaped decline; since the non-state-owned economy had not occupied great shares of the market at that time, the rapid decline of state-owned economic outputs would lead to the decline of overall economic outputs. However, the statistical relation between $d - p^*$ and G also suggests that state-owned enterprises exposed to soft constraints are extremely insensitive to the interest rate. The rise of the interest rate evidently will not inhibit their credit demands and the decrease of the interest rate will not stimulate their credit demands significantly. In other words, the interest rate is nearly neutral to state-owned enterprises.

2 Introduction of the institutional factor

Since the existing model of money demand failed to explain the situation in China, the only choice is to re-build the function of money demand in China. The model for the theory of financial deepening was established based on neoclassicism according to the prior discussions, while the situation of China shall be explained from the perspective of institutional changes. Therefore, to adapt the model for the theory of financial deepening to the situation in China, it is necessary to revise and expand the model to a great extent and, particularly, increase the relevant institutional variables.

As a matter of fact, many domestic and foreign economists have been trying to create a function of money demand that reflects the characteristics of the transitional economy in China in recent years. The two most representative models proved upon statistical verification are the model of Yi Gang (1996a) and the model of Qin Duo (1997). Compared to researches of other scholars, researches of Yi Gang and Qin Duo attached more importance to the factor of institutional changes.

Giving consideration to the factor of institutional changes, Yi Gang (1996a) proposed the model of money demand before the reform (1952–1978) and the model of money demand since the reform (1979–1989). Also based on the equation of exchange $MV = Py$, we obtain the equation of $m = (1/V)y = ky$, and $m = M/P$. Applying the natural logarithm in the equation and replacing $\ln k$ with C and based on $k = 1/V$, the following model of money demand before the reform in acquired:

$$\ln m = C + \ln y + D \tag{4.3}$$

D in the equation is a dummy variable. Based on the equation (4.3), Yi Gang considered the monetization of the Chinese economy as a factor of institutional change and thus once revised the equation of exchange as $MV = \lambda yP$, while λ is the proportion of the monetized economy. Then he got the model of money demand after the reform:

$$\ln m = C + \ln y + \ln \lambda + D \tag{4.4}$$

By conducting a regression estimate on equation (4.3) and (4.4), it can be seen that the income elasticity coefficient before the reform was close to 1, demonstrating that the practical per-capital income and per-capita money demand were increasing simultaneously. After the reform, the income elasticity coefficient significantly dropped to about 0.75 due to the introduction of the factor of monetization, suggesting that the factor of monetization could explain the growth of money demand. Yi Gang applied the percentage of urban population as an approximate variable to the process of monetization that each 1% growth of the percentage of urban population (i.e., the level of monetization) would result in growth of practical money demand by 0.81%–0.95%. Considering the opportunity cost of holding cash, Yi Gang put forward a new function of money demand:

$$\ln m = C + \ln(rs) + \pi + \ln(UP) \tag{4.5}$$

In equation (4.5), Yi Gang replaced y with the practical retail sales rs, replaced λ with the percentage of urban population (UP) and increased the estimated inflation rate π (i.e., the opportunity cost of holding cash). Based on the regression estimate with the data between 1983 and 1989, if representing m with the practical per-capita money demand M^w_2 calculated upon the mixed price index, the following result of double logarithmic verification is achieved:

$$\ln M^w_2 = 1.231 + 0.653 \ln(rs) - 0.004\pi + 0.511\ln(UP)$$
$$(3.13) \quad (4.64) \quad (-2.12) \quad (5.07)$$
$$R^2 = 0.933, DW = 1.507$$

Seen from the aforementioned result of verification, the income elasticity coefficient of per-capita retail sales is 0.65, the urban population elasticity is 0.51 and the influence of the estimated inflation rate on money demand is insignificant.[6] In conclusion, two major factors would affect money demand in China, the growth of incomes and the process of monetization. It shall be noted that the factor of the interest rate was not incorporated in Yi Gang's function of money demand, which seemed greatly relevant to the neutrality of the interest rate as discussed prior. As explained by Yi Gang, the interest rate in China was under strict control by the government and was fixed at a level much lower than the point of equilibrium, so it could not reflect the opportunity cost of holding cash. A summary of Yi Gang's model of money demand is presented here as for M-S initial model. Yi Gang (1995) presented an expression of the function of money demand:

$$m^d = f(y, r, \lambda, \pi, b) \tag{4.6}$$

In the equation, $m^d = M/P$, y is the gross national product, r means the interest rate, λ indicates the monetization index, π is the estimate of the inflation rate and b represents the international balance of payments. If we adhere to the hypothesis of the closed economy, b could be removed, and if r is replaced by the practical interest rate, $r - \pi$ can be calculated, which will be replaced by $d - p^*$. Then the equation (4.6) can be expressed as:

$$m^d = f(y, \lambda, d - p^*) \tag{4.7}$$

Since the factor of the interest rate is basically neutral, $d - p^*$ can also be removed. The function of money demand can be further simplified as:

$$m^d = f(y, \lambda) \tag{4.8}$$

In the equation, $\partial f/\partial y > 0$ and $\partial f/\partial \lambda > 0$. Yi Gang's model of money demand that stresses the factor of monetization exactly corresponds to discussions in Chapter 2 of this book. However, the full connotation of the function of money demand in China can hardly be explained merely with the factor of monetization. For example, only based on the factor of monetization, it is difficult to answer the question of why people's money demand is still rising sharply when the effect of the factor of monetization is diminishing along with the further development of monetization.

Qin Duo (1997) attempted to extend the general theory of money demand[7] by introducing some new institutional factors. In his opinion, the general theory of money demand only described the general law by abstracting concrete factors such as all kinds of economic systems and the economic development stage, which might oversimplify a complicated issue if it is applied to explain money demand after the reform in China. Therefore, the general theory of money demand needed to be extended to adapt to the transition of China. Qin Duo mainly considered following institutional factors when extending the general model of money demand: (1) the inhibitory investment demand due to the planned control; (2) the excessive fund demand led by soft constraints by the planning system; and (3) the supernormal demand on money due to marketization driven by the reform (i.e., the money demand resulting from the so-called factor of monetization). The extended model shall be:

$$m = f(y, p, R_I, R_F, R_L) \tag{4.9}$$

In the equation, y and p respectively represent the current income and price level, R_I is the interest rate, R_F means the ratio of state-owned industrial outputs during the process of monetization and R_L refers to the loan-deposit ratio under soft constraints. Among the three major institutional factors mentioned here, the investment demand involved in the first factor is represented with the variable of the interest rate. As the investment demand in China is subject to inhibitions, the variable of the interest rate is weak in explaining the function of the money demand. The third factor actually equals λ in Yi Gang's model. Yi Gang applied the measurable proportion of urban population (*UP*) as the approximate variable to λ, while Qin Duo used the ratio of state-owned industrial outputs in the gross industrial outputs. Further investigation is needed to determine which approximate variable holds the greater explanatory power. In terms of the issue concerned with here, the important thing is affirming the significant influence of the process of monetization on money demand during the transition instead of deciding which approximate variable should be used. In this regard, both Qin Duo's model and Yi Gang's model are satisfying.

Qin Duo's model is uniquely characterized by a brand new institutional factor introduced, that is, the second factor listed earlier, the excessive fund demand led by soft constraints by the planning system. In equation (4.9), he used the measurable loan-deposit ratio of state-owned banks R_L. This is undoubtedly a very important institutional factor. However, giving special consideration to demonstrating the stability of money demand in China since the reform and money derived from demands, Qin Duo eliminated the factor along with the variable of the interest rate when conducting metrological verification on the mode and the long-run equilibrium relationship of money demand. This is because the soft constraint reflected by violent changes of the total credit speed had stimulated the growth of money demand, but the soft constraint of the total credit would see increasingly slow growth along with deepening of the reform and its power to lead to excessive money demand would decrease, according to the recursive estimation of the model. However, the facts show that the loan-deposit ratio of state-owned banks still stayed high owing to financial support based on the soft constraint. Self-owned funds of state-owned banks accounted for only 4.34% of the total assets in 1996. As state-owned banks still largely depended on deposits, the power to lead to excessive money demand still existed. Moreover, the soft constraint could be divided into the financial soft constraint of state-owned enterprises and the credit soft constraint of state-owned banks, both of which brought pressures on expansion of monetary supply of the state (the so-called reversed mechanism of the pressure). However, the pressure on monetary supply did not result in severe inflation, as the growth of *M2* driven by money demand of the household sector covered the pressure on basic money supply (particularly *M0*) of the central bank. According to statistics in Table 4.2, the average growth rate of *M2* in the 12 years between 1985 and 1996 reached 27.31%, 4.58% higher than the average growth rate of *M0* of 22.73%. The growth of *M2* was far more stable than *M0* in this period. Based on Table 4.3, except 1984 to 1985, 1988 to 1989 and the year 1993, *M0/M2* has kept at a low level in China, constantly declined after 1993 and reached

Table 4.2 Monetary growth of China: 1985–1996

(%)												
	1985	*1986*	*1987*	*1988*	*1989*	*1990*	*1991*	*1992*	*1993*	*1994*	*1995*	*1996*	*Average*
M0	24.7	23.3	19.4	46.7	9.8	12.8	20.2	36.5	35.3	24.3	8.2	11.6	22.73
M1	5.8	28.1	16.2	22.5	6.3	20.2	23.2	35.7	38.9	26.8	16.8	18.9	21.62
M2	25.4	29.3	24.2	21.0	18.3	28.0	27.1	30.7	24.0	49.0	29.5	21.2	27.31

Data source: *China Financial Outlook* (1994, 1997), Table 3.1 of the Chinese edition of this book.

Table 4.3 M0/M2 of China: 1978–1996

(Billion Yuan)			
	M0	*M2*	*M0/M2*
1978	21.20	115.91	0.18
1979	26.77	145.81	0.18
1980	34.62	194.29	0.18
1981	39.63	223.45	0.18
1982	43.91	258.98	0.17
1983	52.98	307.50	0.17
1984	79.21	414.63	0.19
1985	98.78	519.89	0.19
1986	121.84	672.10	0.18
1987	145.45	834.97	0.17
1988	213.40	1,009.96	0.21
1989	234.40	1,194.96	0.20
1990	264.40	1,529.37	0.17
1991	317.80	1,943.99	0.16
1992	433.60	2,540.21	0.17
1993	586.47	3,150.10	0.19
1994	728.86	4,692.35	0.16
1995	788.53	6,075.00	0.13
1996	880.20	7,361.33	0.12

Data source: Table 8.1 of Yi Gang (1996a), Table 3.1 of the Chinese edition of this book, Table 3.6 of *China Financial Outlook* (1997).

only 0.120 in 1996. If calculated upon the ratio of the increment, it has dropped even faster. As shown in Table 4.4, the ratio of increment of *M0* to *M2* in 1996 was only 0.07.

As a matter of fact, the soft constraint of budgets played a very significant role in the growth of money demand and constituted the key variable to explaining the money demand of China under the gradual reform, the same as the level of monetization in Yi Gang's model. The difference lies in that the factor of monetization

Table 4.4 Annual increment of M0 and M2 of China: 1978–1996

	(Billion Yuan)		
	ΔM0	ΔM2	ΔM0/ΔM2
1978	1.66	5.18	0.32
1979	5.57	29.90	0.19
1980	7.85	48.48	0.16
1981	5.01	29.16	0.17
1982	4.28	35.53	0.12
1983	9.07	48.52	0.19
1984	26.23	107.13	0.24
1985	19.57	105.26	0.19
1986	23.06	152.21	0.15
1987	23.61	162.87	0.14
1988	67.95	175.02	0.39
1989	21.00	185.00	0.11
1990	30.00	334.41	0.09
1991	53.40	414.62	0.13
1992	115.80	596.22	0.19
1993	152.87	609.89	0.25
1994	142.39	1,542.25	0.09
1995	59.67	1,382.65	0.04
1996	91.67	1,286.33	0.07

Data source: Table 8.1 of Yi Gang (1996a), Table 3.1 of the Chinese edition of this book, Table 3.6 of *China Financial Outlook* (1997).

tended to reflect the initial conditions of money demand in China, while the soft constraint revealed the internal structure and features of money demand in China in a more profound way. We noticed the subtle logical connection between the factor of the soft constraint and the inhibitory factor of investment demand. As stressed several times, the growth of the state-owned economy (particularly the state-owned industrial outputs) must be stable in order to avoid the J-shaped curve of economic growth during gradual reform. The stable fund supply must be guaranteed to maintain growth, which would mainly depend on financial support due to the decline of fiscal capacity. China enjoyed relatively favorable financial conditions during the reform as the process of monetization provided adequate gains from monetization including the large amount of financial surpluses, but the financial surpluses had to be put in the accounts of state-owned banks before the favorable financial conditions were successfully transformed to satisfy the fund demand of state-owned enterprises subject to the soft constraint. Therefore, it further required inhibiting people's opportunity cost on holding deposits certificates of state-owned banks, in other words, inhibiting their investment demand (on the condition of restricting development of other financial instruments). From this point of view, the soft constraint played a special role in the growth of money demand during transition in China. Moreover, the soft constraint also exerted influence on the insignificance of the factor of the interest rate. Qin Duo's model of money demand can be revised as:

$$m = f(y, d - p^*, R_P R_L) \tag{4.10}$$

The $d - p^*$ in this equation is acquired by combining p and R_I in equation (4.9). As Qin Duo considered $d - p^*$ insignificant, it could be removed. The result should be as follows:

$$m = f(y, R_P R_L) \tag{4.11}$$

In the equation, $\partial f / \partial R_F < 0$, $\partial f / \partial R_L > 0$, $\partial f / \partial y > 0$. Compared to Yi Gang's model, the odel of Qin Duo (4.11) added a new variable, R_L. Although it was eliminated during metrological verification on the mode and the long-run equilibrium relationship of money demand, it was very meaningful to point out the variable and confirm its role in stimulating money demand during the transition. Qin Duo's model can be regarded as an extension and supplement to Yi Gang's model.

However, it is necessary to reconsider whether the ratio of state-owned industrial outputs, R_F, could be applied to represent the factor of monetization in Qin Duo's model. The decline of the ratio of state-owned industrial outputs demonstrates the higher level of monetization, but the ratio should not drop too fast as it will lead to J-shaped economic growth, as mentioned earlier. Therefore, the sufficient credit support shall be rendered to protect the ratio of state-owned industrial outputs from decreasing too fast, which means that the loan-deposit ratio of state-owned banks, R_L, should be maintained at a relatively high level and ultimately requires the stable growth of people's money demand (particularly deposits in state-owned banks). The increase of money demand is realized upon the condition of rise of the monetization level. Therefore, it is an obvious paradox. It is inappropriate to adopt the ratio of state-owned industrial outputs as the approximate variable to the factor of monetization.

3   Model expansion: considering the factor of state capacity

Generally speaking, the models of Yi Gang and Qin Duo introduced two important institutional variables and made vital corrections to the initial M-S model (although they might not be aware of this). Their models well explained the money demand in the reform of China. However, there are still some problems in the models of Yi Gang and Qin Duo as follows. First, although it is correct to remove the factor of the interest rate from the model (Qin Duo's model) or not introduce the factor to the model (Yi Gang's model), they have ignored the institutional factor behind the insignificance of the factor of the interest rate. As mentioned prior, state-owned economic outputs during the gradual reform mainly depended on support by financial subsidies. As financial subsidies required a low cost, state-owned banks only applied a low interest rate for loans to state-owned enterprises. Meanwhile, state-owned banks also needed a low financing cost to sustain their capability in financial support, that is, a low interest rate of deposits (a relatively low interest rate compared to the equilibrium interest rate instead of an absolutely low interest rate). The regression estimation in equation (4.1) and equation (4.2) exactly demonstrates that the lower practical interest rate of deposits played a special role in stimulating deposits and economic growth (mainly outputs of state-owned enterprises) during the reform. The positive role of the low interest rate to economic growth can be explained by neoclassicism, in that the low interest rate stimulated investment and the growth of investment boosted the growth of outputs. However, the fact that the lower practical interest rate of deposits (i.e., decline of the money yield) promoted people to voluntarily (at least seemed voluntary) hold more cash in hand (or deposits certificate) could not be explained merely through the inhibitory investment demand (opportunity cost) or the general theory. More significantly, the powerful financial control and guarantee to state-owned banks by the government actually covered people's losses incurred by the low yield of cash in hand. The low currency risk and high currency gains could be an alternative to each other for savers. Therefore, in terms of the function of money demand in China, another important institutional variable, state capacity (i.e., people's confidence in the state), must be considered.[8] During the gradual reform in China, the factor of state capacity has practically replaced the factor of the interest rate as an important variable to stimulate the growth of money demand. In this sense, savers were more inclined to purchase deposit certificates of state-owned banks although many other financial organizations were doing everything possible to attract them, which obviously showed their willingness and preference for the factor of safety.

Second, both Yi Gang and Qin Duo's models pointed out the impact of inflation on money demand, as inflation would be considered a kind of opportunity cost of holding cash. Nevertheless, the impact of inflation was unobvious in the function of money demand in China, which further strengthened the role of state capacity. Although the government could maintain the demand on savings (or cash in hand) by inhibiting the investment demand, it could not change people's choice between the transaction demand and savings demand. In case of the sharp rise of inflation, people would be inclined to exchange material objects (wealth) with money, as proved by several times of panic buying and run on banks in the 1980s. However, with its strong capacity, the state was able to control inflation within a certain level and keep people's confidence in holding cash (or deposits certificates). Therefore, the insignificant role of the factor of interest rate and inflation in the model of money demand in China could be attributed to the significant role of the factor of state capacity.

Third, the factor of state capacity enables the integration and communication between the factor of monetization and the factor of soft constraint. The factor of soft constraint requires state-owned banks to maintain a high loan-deposit ratio, while the high loan-deposit ratio demands people's interest in deposit certificates of state-owned banks. A financial system under the state monopoly is obviously needed to put financial surpluses that are mainly driven by the factor of monetization (based on development of the non-state-owned economy and the corresponding economic growth) into deposit accounts of state-owned banks. As pointed out prior, the state-owned financial property right form under the state monopoly has played a key part in absorbing savings from monetization. In other words, only when the state is capable of controlling the state-owned financial property right form can monetization be transformed to be the huge amount of deposits in state-owned banks and support the high loan-deposit ratio. Therefore, the factor of monetization and soft constraint stressed in Yi Gang and Qin Duo's model only constituted the necessary condition for maintaining money demand, while the factor of state capacity was the sufficient condition for the growth of money demand. Based on discussions in Section 2, Point 3 of Chapter 3, the strong enough state capacity (P^g) could guarantee the great amount of D^h; the great amount of D^h could guarantee the growth of L^s; and the growth of L^s would finally promote the stable growth of G, the in-system outputs.

By combining Yi Gang and Qin Duo's model, we can acquire the following equation:

$$M^d = F(y, R_p, R_L) \tag{4.12}$$

Since λ and R_F both are factors of monetization and λ is more appropriate to represent the factor of monetization as discussed prior, R_F can be incorporated into λ. If considering the factor of state capacity and incorporating R_F into P^g (P^g actually also incorporates the variable of $d - p^*$ and V, the vector of the opportunity cost of holding cash as defined by Edward Shaw), the extended function of money demand of China can be obtained:

$$M^d = F(y, P^g) \tag{4.13}$$

All partial derivatives in this equation are positive. It is important to note that the influence of the factor of monetization and state capacity will gradually decrease or become stable and the role of $d - p^*$ will be increasingly important, along with the further development of reform and reinforced marketing effects. It suggests that the model of money demand in China shall be exposed to constant revisions during the process of the gradual reform.

The equation (4.13) is illustrated in Figure 4.1 in a more intuitive manner. The equation supposes that the curve of money demand at the beginning of the reform was m^d_0, the curve of money supply was m^s_0, and the amount of money demand was $\bar{m}^d_0$, and it further supposes that the interest rate was kept above the inhibitory $(d - p^*)_0$ and the money demand equaled the money supply. Since the reform began, people's money yield (y) had been rapidly increasing and the corresponding transaction demand had been sharply rising, so the state expanded the money supply. As a result, the money demand increased from the original $\bar{m}^d_0$ to $\bar{m}^d_0 + \bar{m}^d_1$, while $\bar{m}^d_1$ referred to the money demand driven by the growth of household income. At the same time, as the previous planned economic system was broken,

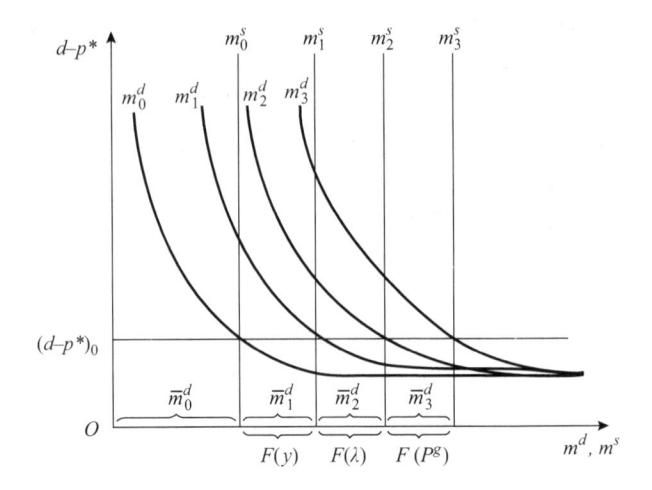

Figure 4.1 The model of money demand in China: during the transition

social and economic exchanges and payment methods have been exposed to great changes and economic monetization has been improved, which further stimulated the growth of money demand in the economy. To satisfy the money demand, the state expanded the money (supply) again. The money demand increased from the original $\bar{m}_0^d + \bar{m}_1^d$ to $\bar{m}_0^d + \bar{m}_1^d + \bar{m}_2^d$. $\bar{m}_2^d$ refers to the money demand driven by the factor of monetization. On this basis, when people's money yield continued increasing, people's money demand mainly in the form of holding deposit certificates of state-owned banks was constantly expanding due to the state's control capacity (including inhibition on investment demand and inflation control). Then money demand further grew from $\bar{m}_0^d + \bar{m}_1^d + \bar{m}_2^d$ to $\bar{m}_0^d + \bar{m}_1^d + \bar{m}_2^d + \bar{m}_3^d$. It is for the convenience of discussion to divide the money demand into different ranges based on the influencing factor in Figure 4.1. In fact, these factors including y, λ and P_g produce effects on money demand jointly during the process of the gradual reform.

Notes

1 See more details of the validation process in Ronald McKinnon (1996, pages 18–27).
2 See more detailed data in the World Bank (1989, page 31).
3 M. Fry had once proposed the revised model of financial development (1988, 1982), but failed to put forward some original ideas. He had drawn more attention with his metrological validations. For example, in statistics of Kitchen, six validations were conducted by Fry.
4 If the consumption factor and inflation are taken into consideration, people would choose immediate consumption instead of holding cashes in case of the lower money yield. However, this situation rarely occurred in China.

5 Zang Xuheng (1995) analyzed and validated the correlativity between the growth rate of deposits and the nominal interest rate of China, while the result suggested the low correlativity between the two, with a correlation coefficient of only 0.114 (page 212). He also established econometric models to research the relationship among residents' consumption, incomes and the interest rate of deposits and between the average propensity to consume and the interest rate. All results showed the extremely small influence of the interest rate. The small effect of the interest rate on consumption also proved its small effect on deposits. Theoretically, neoclassical economics generally believe that changes in the interest rate have an affirmatory influence on consumption (or deposits), i.e., when the interest rate increases, consumption would reduce and deposits would grow, and when the interest rate drops, consumption would increase and deposits would decrease. The initial M-S model is attributed to neoclassicism. Later, some Western economists (mainly Keynesianism economists such as Edward Shapiro and Cardner Ackley) discovered that deposits showed minor response to changes in the interest rate. According to Edward Shapiro (1985), the influence of the interest rate on deposits was determined by the balance of power between the substitution effect and income effect, so a simple systematic relation could not be established between the total savings of an individual and the interest rate. Therefore, many economists held an agnostic position on this issue. They admitted that changes of the interest rate might change the total savings of an individual at any level of disposable income, but the changes of the savings rate might show the same or the different direction to changes of the interest rate (pages 205–207). In a word, the neoclassical school stressed the interest rate as the most important factor affecting deposits, but the theory of deposits of Keynesianism transferred the focus from the interest rate to income. Apparently, the situation in China provided evidence to the latter opinion, although the causes leading to the situation might be different.

6 Zang Xuheng (1995) conducted a regression analysis over the lagging estimated price index based on total household consumption expenditure between 1978 and 1991 and analyzed the effect of price expectation on consumption expenditure. The result indicated that the price index showed no statistical significance in the regression and therefore had nearly no influence on the average consumption propensity (page 214). It can be deducted that the price expectation will not exert a significant effect on deposits (a kind of money demand).

7 The so-called general theory of money demand here is expressed as $m - p = k + \alpha y + BRc$, with the income elasticity of money demand as α, the coefficient vector of the cost of holding cashes as B and the cost of holding cases as Rc.

8 According to the World Bank (1996b), the high rate of savings demonstrated people's high trust in the financial strength of the banking system and the lack of alternatives of financial assets for most organizations and families (page 27). Both factors are relevant to the state's control capacity.

5 Transitional arrangements of the financial system

1 Which kind of financial institutional arrangement is favorable for savings mobilization during the transition?

I Comparative advantages of monopolistic financial arrangements

The discussion on the function of money demand of China in Chapter 4 reaches a conclusion that the deposits of China (a kind of money demand) are basically irrelevant to the interest rate of deposits under the transitional economy and that money demand is expanded mainly based on the factor of monetization and particularly state capacity. However, Chapter 4 does not describe how state capacity affects money demand and especially the growth of deposits in detail. There are some important mechanisms and organizations between state capacity and growth of money demand, that is, financial institutional arrangements. Although involved in the previous discussions, financial institutional arrangements are only incidentally mentioned in discussions of other issues. This chapter attempts to establish certain connections among factors such as state capacity, financial institutional arrangements, growth of money demand and so forth here.

It is noteworthy that this function of money demand in China incorporating the variable of state capacity only explains why people are willing to hold money (including the deposit certificates of state-owned banks) under transitional conditions (i.e., the low interest rate compared to the equilibrium interest rate), but fails to explain why state-owned banks supply deposit certificates in such a large scale that exceeds theoretical boundaries under the condition of very low ratio of self-owned capitals (only 4.34% in 1996) as it is not free to supply deposit certificates. It is imaginable that the provision of deposit certificates would be stopped at a certain point of equilibrium (where the marginal revenue of the provision of deposit certificates equals the marginal cost) under normal market-oriented financial conditions. Even considering the factor of low interest rate of deposits in China, why the provision can far exceed the point of equilibrium is still inexplicable. Without an answer to this question, it will be difficult to establish a credible logical connection between state capacity and the growth of deposits.

Under the transitional economy, the pure market-oriented financial system is unable to provide sufficient money supply (such as deposit certificates). In other words, upon the hypothesis that people are willing to hold money, the demand will exceed the supply of money if there are not appropriate transitional financial arrangements, when the resources of savings cannot be fully mobilized and the economy under transition (particularly the state-owned economy) will see J-shaped decline due to a lack of timely and vigorous financial support. Therefore, a special transitional financial institutional arrangement is needed for the economy in the transition. The existence of the special financial institutional arrangement under the state monopoly or state control in China exactly provides sufficient money at low cost for the economy in transition and thus timely realizes people's money demand.

If a competitive financial institutional arrangement that is not owned by the state or not directly controlled by the state was rapidly introduced to a transitional economy, the financial institutions would only absorb household deposits based on an equilibrium interest rate. If the assumed equilibrium interest rate was higher than the interest rate confirmed by the state, all financial institutions would be up against the high cost of deposit certificates and would have their scale of deposits restricted. Since people would show greater preference to savings upon the high equilibrium interest rate according to the initial M-S model, people's savings demand could hardly be satisfied in this case. More importantly, the high equilibrium interest rate for state-owned financial institutions indicated that the state would have to pay the greater cost to mobilize savings and provide financial support to the state-owned economy.

By comparison, the financial institutional arrangement under state monopoly features evident comparative advantages in controlling the cost of deposit certificates and expanding the scale of savings, which can be illustrated with Figure 5.1.

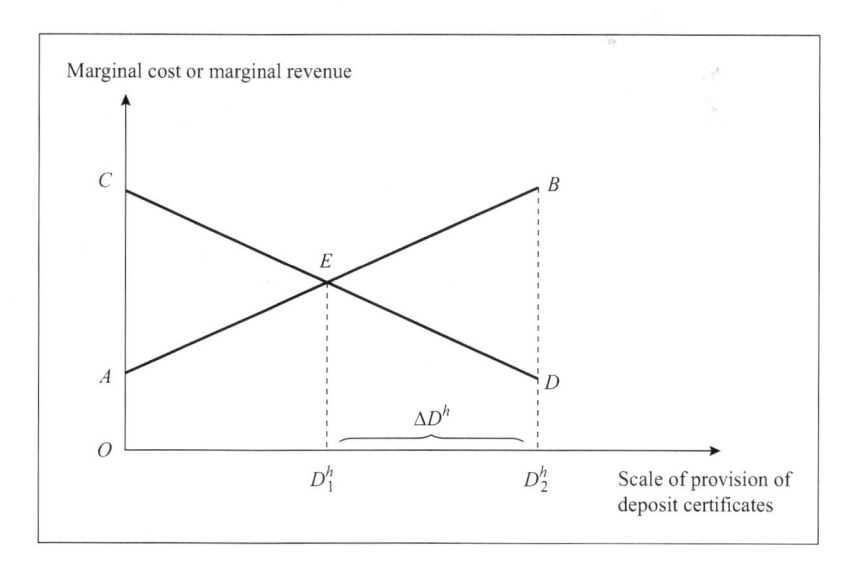

Figure 5.1 Comparative advantages of the monopoly financial system in mobilizing savings

In Figure 5.1, the horizontal axis indicates the amount of supply of deposit certificates (and also indicates the level of deposits mobilization), while the vertical axis refers to the marginal cost or marginal revenue of the provision of deposit certificates. Line AB is the curve of the marginal cost of the provision of deposit certificates, and Line CD is the curve of the marginal revenue of the provision of deposit certificates. If financial control by the state and the restriction on access to the financial market had been relaxed at the beginning of the reform, a competitive financial institutional structure would have been formed rapidly. In such a competitive financial institutional structure, the supply of deposit certificates would depend on the comparison between the marginal cost and marginal revenue. In Figure 5.1, the scale of deposit certificates in a competitive financial institutional structure is only OD^h_1. Theoretically, it is apparently far from satisfying the great demand of the transitional economy on savings. Figure 5.1 can be compared to Figure 3.5 here. The supply of deposit certificates in OD^h_1 could only support the loan scale of OL^S_1 and the low economic growth rate G_1 (in-system outputs growth) in the function of in-system outputs based on a fixed proportion. Interestingly, the financial support (loans) rendered by a competitive financial institutional structure is only OL^S_1 according to Figure 3.5 (c), which exactly corresponds to the provision of deposit certificates OD^h_1 in a competitive financial institutional structure. In any case, a competitive financial institutional structure is unfavorable for the mobilization of savings and stable growth of in-system outputs.

However, in the financial institutional framework of state monopoly, the scale of provision of deposit certificates will exceed OD^h_1 and attain OD^h_2. This is because the monopolistic financial system complies with the "aggregate principle" of the total cost equaling the total revenue instead of the "marginal principle" in providing deposit certificates. As shown in Figure 5.1, when the level of savings mobilization is OD^h_2, the area of total revenue $OCDD^h_2$ equals the area of total cost $OABD^h_2$. Compared to Figure 3.5, it can be seen that the scale of provision of deposit certificates in OD^h_2 exactly corresponds to the loan provision OL^S_2 and the higher level of in-system outputs G_2 in the function of in-system outputs based on a fixed proportion. Then, ΔD^h in Figure 5.1 is the comparative advantage of the monopolistic financial institutional arrangement in mobilizing savings in the transitional economy. This result further demonstrates the appropriateness of the stress on state capacity in the model of money demand proposed in Chapter 4. Chapter 3 emphasized that the difference in savings constituted a fundamental cause for different performances of the transitional economy in the Soviet Union, Eastern Europe and China, which is also theoretically supported by the discussion here. It can be concluded that the difference in economic growth during the transition depended on the difference in savings, and the difference in savings depended on the difference in the transitional financial institutional structure, while the difference in the transitional financial institutional structure depended on the difference in state capacity.

II Performance of the mixed financial institutional arrangement in mobilizing savings

Aforementioned discussions touched on the different performances of the purely competitive and monopolistic financial institutional arrangement in mobilizing savings. Here we can further imagine a kind of mixed financial institutional arrangement in the transitional economy where the competitive non-state-owned financial system and the state-owned financial system (non-monopolistic) co-exist. Then, what performance would this kind of financial arrangement achieve in mobilizing savings? Theoretically, if free access to the credit market was allowed since the beginning of the reform, the newly entered non-state-owned financial institutions would encounter a curve of the higher marginal cost of providing deposit certificates. This was because, on one hand, non-state-owned financial institutions possibly would be exposed to interference by non-market factors due to the incomplete market system at the initial stage of the reform, and, on the other hand, non-state-owned financial institutions tended to apply a higher interest rate to loans since the confidential relationship in credit transactions could not be established right off, which suggested a greater default (moral) risk during the provision of credits as well as the larger information cost that non-state-owned financial institutions should pay. Therefore, the marginal cost of providing deposit certificates would rise.

As shown in Figure 5.2, the curve of the marginal cost rises from the original AB to $A'B'$. We suppose that the curve of marginal revenue has no change. The

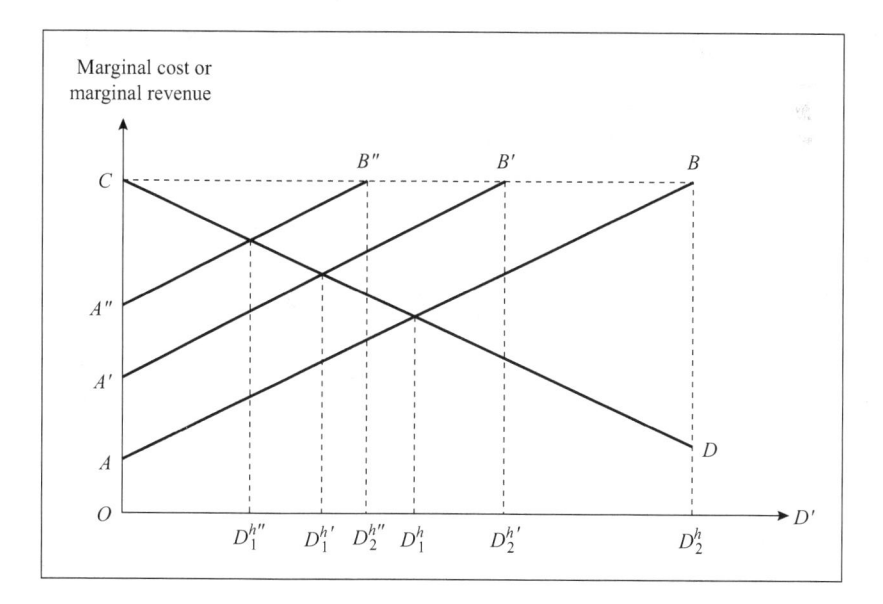

Figure 5.2 Provision of deposit certificates under the mixed financial institutional arrangement

downward change of the curve of the marginal revenue and the upward change of the curve of the marginal cost exert the same influence on the scale of provision of deposit certificates. Therefore, the scale of provision of deposit certificates would reduce from the original OD^h_1 to the smaller $OD^{h\prime}_1$. Moreover, state-owned financial institutions (such as state-owned banks) would also face the higher equilibrium interest rate of deposits and the corresponding higher interest rate of loans due to the mixed financial institutional arrangement. However, state-owned enterprises, the major object of the credit funds of state-owned banks, would find it difficult to accept the higher interest rate of loans. Therefore, the interest rate of loans of state-owned banks could hardly achieve the equilibrium level in the bargaining among all relevant interested parties. As a result, the interest rate of deposits could hardly be maintained at a high level because state-owned banks would suffer a higher marginal cost if so. The more interesting thing is that if state-owned banks lowered the interest rate of deposits corresponding to the interest rate of loans, the demand on deposit certificates of state-owned banks would drop as people would switch to hold deposit certificates of non-state-owned financial institutions of a higher interest rate upon the rapid development of non-state-owned finance and the establishment of their reputation. To avoid the loss of deposit certificates, state-owned banks would have to maintain the interest rate of deposits at the equilibrium level. Under these circumstances, the interest rate of loans would drop far away from that of deposits. In this case, the state would be urged to allocate more funds as subsidies to state-owned banks, or the central bank would be pressed to render more re-loans, very likely resulting in people's inflation expectation. Then the scale of provision of deposit certificates of state-owned banks would apparently rely on state capacity to bear these subsidies. Anyhow, the deposit certificates of state-owned banks would see the same curve of the marginal cost as those of non-state-owned banks. Based on the aggregate principle of providing deposit certificates, the practical scale of provision of deposit certificates of state-owned banks would drop from the previous OD^h_2 under the monopolistic state to $OD^{h\prime}_2$, as shown in Figure 5.2. Besides, it is highly possible that the overall scale of deposit certificates provided under the mixed financial institutional system is smaller than the scale under the monopolistic financial institutional system, that is, $OD^{h\prime}_1 + OD^{h\prime}_2 < OD^h_2$.

Even if the sum of $OD^{h\prime}_1$ and $OD^{h\prime}_2$ could be equal to or greater than OD^h_2, the situation would not last long. This is because if $OD^{h\prime}_2 < OD^h_2$, the financial support (or financial subsidies) would be minor, which could hardly guarantee the stable growth of state-owned economic outputs during the transition. A chain of reactions would arise in case of decline of in-system outputs. The most serious is that the state treasury mainly depending on taxes submitted by the state-owned sector would face more severe conditions. It would necessarily lead to monetary expansion (the expansion of savings replaced the base monetary expansion to a great extent under the monopolistic financial institutional conditions), when people would show strong inflation expectation and decline of confidence in holding money and the money demand would reduce correspondingly. In this case, the provision of deposit certificates would see a higher curve of the marginal cost

$A''B''$, while state-owned banks would need to pay a higher cost (for example, banks would need to pay a higher fixed cost such as office expenses, salaries, welfare etc. due to decline of deposits) to further mobilize savings. Ultimately, the provision of deposit certificates of state-owned banks would be further lowered to $OD^{h''}_2$ as shown in Figure 5.2, and the decline of deposits would lead to further expansion of base money, forming a vicious cycle. In this sense, the overall provision of deposit certificates in the mixed financial institutional arrangement might be no lower than in the monopolistic financial system at the start, but the situation would not last long. When the provision of deposit certificates of state-owned banks dropped along with the reduction of people's money demand, the provision in the mixed arrangement would see significant decline. If considering that the inflation expectation generated within the system would necessarily exert negative influence on the provision of deposit certificates of non-state-owned finance (i.e., the scale of provision of deposit certificates reduced from $OD^{h'}_1$ to $OD^{h'}_{1)}$), the overall provision of deposit certificates in the mixed financial system would be further cut down.

2   About "financial restraint"

I   Re-exploration of the factor of state capacity

Since the monopolistic financial institutional arrangement is more favorable for mobilizing savings in the transitional economy, it is a logical deduction to maintain and expand the institutional arrangement. Then, it needs to involve the factor of state capacity based on previous discussions. According to the function of money demand in China proposed prior, the practical interest rate barely exerts any influence on providing and purchasing deposit certificates (money demand) when state capacity is involved. It means that in the monopolistic financial institutional arrangement, the state can sell deposit certificates at a lower practical interest rate without affecting the scale of savings.[1] Since state-owned banks no longer encounter the equilibrium interest rate as they do in the mixed financial institutional arrangement, the cost of providing deposit certificates is lowered correspondingly. As indicated in Figure 5.2, the curve of the marginal cost returns to AB again from $A''B''$ (or $A'B'$), and the scale of provision of deposit certificates is restored to the higher OD^h_2. This can be explained in a more intuitive way through Figure 5.3.

Seen from Figure 5.3, SD, the curve representing the provision of deposit certificates, and DD, the curve of demand on deposit certificates, intersect each other at Point E_0 under normal circumstances. $\overline{d - p^*}$ at this time is the equilibrium interest rate and OD_1 is the equilibrium savings scale. As discussed prior, D_1 cannot satisfy the requirement on mobilizing savings in the transitional economy, so the scale of savings mobilized shall be further improved. Theoretically, suppose that there is enough demand on deposit certificates in the economy. In this case, the curve SD needs to be moved upward, that is, applying a higher interest rate $(d - p^*)_2$, to attract savers so that the scale of savings can be expanded to the greater OD_2. This is the logic of the initial M-S model. However, based on the

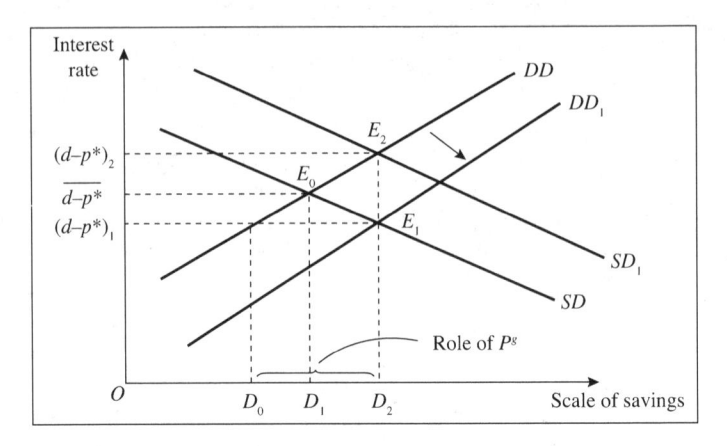

Figure 5.3 Expansion of savings on the condition of low interest rate

function of money demand proposed before, once the factor of state capacity is involved in the transition of China, the scale of savings is basically free from the influence of the interest rate, and state-owned banks can provide more deposit certificates (greater than the equilibrium savings scale) at a lower cost (i.e., the lower interest rate). In Figure 5.3, under general conditions, the lower interest rate $(d - p^*)_1$ would result in a surplus of supply of deposit certificates and insufficient demand on deposit certificates (with the gap of $OD_2 - OD_0$), and the strength contrast would promote the interest rate to rise to $\overline{d - p}^*$. However, when the factor of state capacity is involved, despite the lower level of $(d - p^*)_1$, the curve of demand on deposit certificates in China abnormally moves downward (from DD to DD_1) and intersects SD, the curve of supply of deposits, at Point E_1 upon a non-equilibrium interest rate. Then, the scale of savings mobilization reaches the greater OD_2. We have every reason to believe that OD_2 equals OD^h_2 in Figure 5.1 or 5.2.

II Is rent the only important thing?

Some economists have paid attention to the condition that the monopolistic financial institutional arrangement could mobilize more savings with a lower practical interest rate. Research of Thomas Hellmann, Kevin Murdock and Joseph Stiglitz (Hellmann et al., 1998) regarded the expansion of savings under the low practical interest rate as a result of financial restraint.[2] They believed it would be more favorable to absorbing savings in a developing economy when the government maintained a monopolistic institutional framework instead of a competitive institutional framework.[3] One of the core issues lies in the incentives for the financial sector to attract deposits. To realize the incentives, it is necessary to create rent opportunities for the financial sector. Then, the government has to guarantee the interest rate of deposits lower than the competitive equilibrium interest rate ([i.e., $(d - p^*)_I$ in Figure 5.3), thus creating rent opportunities. As pointed out prior, banks will see a curve of the lower marginal cost for the low interest rate of deposits. Apparently, the financial sector can acquire rents by simply increasing deposits when the interest rate of deposits is lower than the competitive equilibrium interest rate. In this way, they have incentives to seek new deposits to expand rents and especially establish organizations in areas where they were not willing to set up branches (such as rural areas) to fully mobilize savings there.

Since rent is so important, the following issue is how to protect rent from dissipation. One major protective measure is to restrict the access to sustain a temporarily monopoly deposit market, which means to apply patent protection for a few entrants in the existing deposit market. We believe that the state-owned bank was one of the few entrants in the deposit market during the transition in China. The government has effectively controlled the dissipation of rent with this strict access restriction. It is important to point out that the non-government financial sector is the main subject that enters the deposit market and acquires rent according to the analysis framework of financial restraint, and the government applies patent protection for them during their access to the market and endows them with the monopoly power. However, the entrant in China was the state-owned bank, which had been the monopolist since the very beginning. In the former condition, rent is given to the non-government financial sector to drive the sector to expand savings, while in the latter situation, the government acquires rent and finds the corresponding internal incentives. Considering the particularity of the transitional economy in China, that is, the extreme significance of the growth of the state-owned economy to the gradual transition and key role of the financial support by state-owned banks, it is very important whether the government has incentives to mobilize more savings. Although rent shall be obtained by the non-government financial sector according to the theory of financial restraint, rent in China was acquired by the governmental financial sector. Considering the difference in the institutional background, the key lies in the fact that the governmental financial sector acquires rent and maintains the incentives and capability to mobilize savings in China. This is an important complement to the analysis framework of financial restraint.

In fact, the aforementioned conclusion can be directly reached from the previous discussion on the mixed financial institutional arrangement. The negative influence of the mixed financial system on deposit certificates is equivalent to the effect of rent dissipation incurred by excessive access to the deposit market, as rent is decided by the balance between $d - p^*$ and $(d - p^*)_I$. Moreover, although the demand on deposits is irrelevant to $d - p^*$, the supply of deposit certificates has a relation with $d - p^*$, since it is directly associated with the cost and incentives of providers of deposit certificates (state-owned banks or the state). It is obvious that state-owned banks will acquire more rents and show greater initiative in providing deposit certificates in cases of lower interest rate of deposits. In addition, state-owned banks provide deposit certificates in compliance with the "aggregate principle", so they can provide more deposit certificates than non-state-owned banks following the marginal principle on equal conditions. Therefore, it is logical to make state-owned banks the major participant of the deposit market and restrict access of non-state-owned banks. It must be noted that although more deposit certificates can be provided based on the aggregate principle, moderate incentives of rents must be supplied as a condition. A higher level of savings mobilization can only be achieved upon both the aggregate principle and rent incentives. The former is a necessary condition, while the latter is the realization condition. The analysis framework of financial restraint only attaches importance to the realization condition but ignores the necessary condition. Even having the incentive of rents, the non-government financial sector would only sell deposit certificates based on the marginal principle, and the incentive of rents would be limited. As a result, $d - p^*$ would not be lowered too much. If the government requests the non-government financial sector to provide more deposit certificates beyond the marginal principle upon the condition of a certain rent, it means that the non-government financial sector will become the financial sector of the government. The huge scale of provision of deposit certificates and the high level of savings mobilization in China cannot be explained by only rent incentives or only the aggregate principle. Both factors are indispensable.

III　Financial support of money and financial support of securities

For the practical demand of the transitional economy on savings mobilization and financial support, the patent protection for state-owned banks providing deposit certificates and the monopoly state-owned financial institutional arrangement are still insufficient. As implied in the function of the money demand in China proposed earlier, the money demand is the decreasing function of the investment demand. In addition to the practical interest rate of deposits, that is, $d - p^*$, the investment demand must also be considered in the factor of state capacity. The monopoly financial institutional arrangement only restricts other financial organizations from entering the deposit market and has no function in inhibiting investment demand. It means that the institutional setting that inhibits the investment demand shall be taken into consideration in the transitional arrangement of the financial system, which is embodied by the restriction on asset substitution in the analysis framework of financial restraint.

　　Thomas Hellmann et al. (1998) had once listed residents' major four choices of assets, including securities, foreign deposits, informal market deposits and inflation hedge. Sticking to the hypothesis of the closed economy,[4] $d - p^*$ is controlled due to state capacity, and the informal market deposits are subject to constraint for the restriction on access of non-state-owned finance; here we mainly focus on the issue of the securities market, in other words, the investment demand. In the opinion of Thomas Hellmann et al., it may be an effective policy to inhibit the development of the bonds and stocks market at the initial stage of financial development and to not emphasize the role of the securities market when the effective banking system is growing; the securities market only becomes increasingly important along with the deepening of the financial system. The securities market would compete with the banking sector on household funds, when monopolistic banks would lose some businesses of the highest profits and their franchise value, leading to the influence over the rent of the banking sector and threats to the stability of the financial system. This is the fundamental cause to inhibit the securities market. At the early stage of institutional changes when savings mobilization is essential to the transitional economy, it is apparently a rational choice to inhibit the investment demand or restrict the asset substitution. In this sense, it is rational to have the state control the scale of the financial market in China. For the state, savings mobilization is more important than adjusting the social structure of financial assets. Moreover, as $d - p^*$ has been kept at a very low level, slight relaxing of the financial market will result in rapid increase of the opportunity cost of people holding money (deposit certificates) and thus will affect their preference for and confidence in holding deposits. More noteworthy, the securities market of China has been expanding at an increasing rate since 1992. The unsettled state shares (or corporate shares) occupied a large proportion of the market (accounting for 64.36% on average of all shares from 1992 to 1996). This part of investment demand was actually the unconventional part of financial growth, which meant the demand was created as promoted by the government. Therefore, it fundamentally featured the same connotation with savings mobilization of state-owned banks. According to the analysis in Section 2, Point 3 of Chapter 3, it would be finally incorporated in financial support. More intuitively, it made no difference with the credit allocation by state-owned banks. In this way, the development of the securities market did not constitute the standard asset substitution in terms of transfer of savings.

Actually, when state or corporate shares take up a greater proportion, the securities market will not constitute standard asset substitution regardless of the scale. In other words, the asset substitution will not exert any influence on the financial support in the transitional economy. The financial support of credits (money) of state-owned banks transformed from deposit certificates and the financial support of securities transformed from the securities market controlled by the government are equivalent to each other for the stable growth of in-system outputs. This situation will only change when non-state-owned securities occupy increasing shares and are free from direct control by the government, in other words, when the real investment demand and asset substitution emerge. From this aspect, it seems that we can understand the true intention of the government controlling the scale of the securities market. In conclusion, the state has done a very good job in both restricting excessive access to the deposit market and controlling investment demand during the reform. In particular, the state has sustained financial support through asset substitution, which has maintained the growth of in-system outputs and reflected the marketization trend of the whole reform, especially the financial reform.

Here financial support (or financial subsidies) are represented with S^b, including the subsidies provided in the form of credits by state-owned banks based on the growth of deposits (expressed with DS^b) and subsidies provided through the securities market under government control (such as stocks allocation) (presented with SS^b).

Since the financial resources that can be mobilized in the economy within a certain period (or the net balance of monetary incomes held by people) are fixed, the following equation can be reached:

$$S^b = \alpha DS^b + (1 - \alpha)SS^b \qquad (0 \le \alpha \le 1) \tag{5.1}$$

It means that DS^b and SS^b show an inversely proportional relationship. But if the sufficient S^b is provided to support the growth of in-system outputs on the whole, the value of α will not be the key to the issue. Based on conditions since the reform, the development of the securities market did not cut down the scale of financial support since the state imposed strict control on the securities market. This was because a part of financial support originally provided through credits was later rendered in the form of securities released by state-owned enterprises. Therefore, if the state was capable controlling the securities market, it could acquire certain forms of financial subsidies and financial support from the market. The analysis framework of financial restraint failed to consider this approach. Nevertheless, once the government relaxed the control over the securities market, that is, if non-state-owned securities entered the market, it would result in the decline of S^b, the same as relaxing the restriction on access to the deposit market. If we use GS to represent the gross scale of the securities market and GS^n for the share of non-state-owned securities and SS^b for the share of state-owned securities, and suppose that the GS is held by the state-owned sector and non-state-owned sector within a certain period as a fixed value, we can reach the following equation:

$$GS = \beta SSb + (1 - \beta)GS^n \qquad (0 \le \beta \le 1) \tag{5.2}$$

Based on equation (5.2),

$$SS^b = \frac{GS - (1 - \beta)GS^n}{\beta} \tag{5.3}$$

Substituting equation (5.3) into equation (5.1),

$$S^b = \alpha DS^b + \left(\frac{1 - \alpha}{\beta}\right)GS - \frac{(1 - \alpha)(1 - \beta)}{\beta}GS^n \tag{5.4}$$

Apparently,

$$\frac{\partial S^b}{\partial GS^n} = -\frac{(1 - \alpha)(1 - \beta)}{\beta}$$

Since $0 \le \alpha \le 1$ and $0 \le \beta \le 1$,

$$\frac{\partial S^b}{\partial GS^n} < 0$$

That is to say that every increase of GS^n by one unit, S^b will reduce by $\frac{(1-\alpha)(1-\beta)}{\beta}$ unit. Therefore, China allowed access of the state-owned economy but restricted access of the non-state-owned economy during the development of the securities market mainly in order to maintain the appropriate scale of S^b. In this way, a very interesting situation could be seen during the financial reform of China, where the access of the non-state-owned economy into the money (or credit) market was restricted to sustain DS^b at a high enough level, and the access of the non-state-owned economy into the securities market was restricted to form a basically monopolistic market structure, thus to sustain SS^b at a high enough level. Moreover, upon existence of the securities market, the condition for the maximum S^b is:

$$\frac{\partial S^b}{\partial GS} = \frac{\partial S^b}{\partial SS^b} \tag{5.5}$$

Then, $\beta = 1$. It means that if $1 - \alpha$ is a given value, with a higher value of β, the reduction of S^b will be smaller along with each increase of GS^n by one unit. Also seen from equation (5.4), with a higher value of α, the influence of the change to β will be smaller. In summary, the basic characteristics of the transitional arrangement of the financial system in China can be concluded as follows: the state adopted the strategy that ensured the leading role of stimulating the growth of deposits (i.e., the money demand in a broader sense) and the supplementary role of moderate expansion of the securities market in order to maintain the growth of in-system outputs during the gradual reform. In other words, the state did its best to confirm a higher value of α, for instance, mainly allowing in-system financial organizations to enter the deposit market, and meanwhile tried to realize a higher value of β in the securities market so that more in-system departments could enter the securities market.

A revised Hicks model can be introduced to describe the aforementioned discussion. Figure 5.4 presents a revised Hicks geometric design, where the

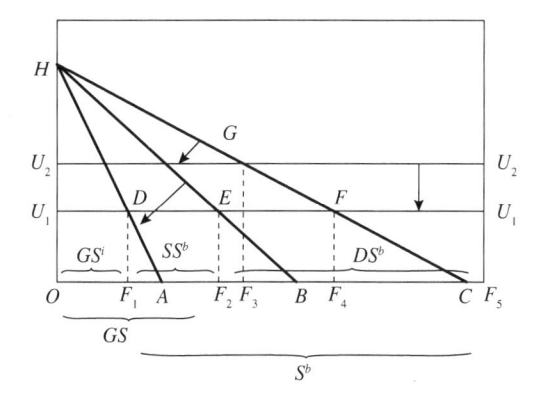

Figure 5.4 A revised Hicks design

horizontal axis indicates financial assets and the vertical axis represents the marginal utility (can be represented with $d - p^*$). U_1U_1 is the curve of the marginal utility of money (deposits) demand under the financial restraint, U_2U_2 is the curve of the marginal utility of money demand in the M-S sense and HC is the curve of the marginal utility of the standard investment demand. According to the initial M-S model, based on the previous discussion, the lower U_1U_1 line will lead to the greater investment demand (OF_4) and smaller money (or deposit certificates) demand (F_4F_5). The marginal utility of the money held in hand shall be improved to make people more willing to hold money (or deposit certificates). If the marginal utility of money held in hand was promoted to U_2U_2, the money (or deposit certificates) demand will be expanded to F_3F_5, and the investment demand will be reduced to OF_3. However, on the condition of financial restraint, not only the marginal utility of money demand is controlled at the lower U_1U_1, but also the marginal utility of investment demand is correspondingly lowered. The original HC utility curve is rotated towards the left to form the utility curve of HB. Under these circumstances, the structure of people's financial assets is decided by the intersection E of the line U_1U_1 and the line HB. Hence, the money demand is expanded to the greater F_2F_5, equal to DS^b in equation (5.1), and the investment demand is reduced to OF_2, equal to GS in equation (5.2). Moreover, a considerable part (i.e., F_1F_2) of OF_2 is held by the state-owned sector and is of high rigidity, being inversely proportional to DS^b (F_2F_5). It makes no difference with DS^b from the perspective of financial support and therefore is free from the strict control by HB, the curve of the marginal utility of the investment demand. As a matter of fact, the investment demand during the transition will encounter HA, a lower and steeper curve of the marginal utility. As the curve of the marginal utility becomes steeper, the influence of changes to the interest rate on securities demand will be smaller. If considering an extreme case where $\beta = 1$, the utility curve HA will be further rotated towards the left and will coincide with the vertical axis, and GS will be fully presented as SS^b. If considering another extreme case where $\alpha = 1$, DS^b will be expanded to OF_5, and financial support (S^b) will be fully presented as the money (deposits) support by state-owned banks.

3 Financial arrangements for out-system growth

I Significance of out-system growth

This discussion explains the special financial institutional arrangement to maintain the constant growth of in-system outputs during the transition. However, it is insufficient from the perspective of the whole institution change and gradual reform. Maintaining the stable growth of in-system outputs was of great significance to the success of the gradual reform at the early stage of the reform, simply because the in-system outputs occupied a higher proportion in the total outputs. But in terms of the long-term process of transition, the most important is whether out-system outputs can acquire rapid growth.

To be specific, the basic significance of maintaining the stable growth of in-system outputs lay in leading the overall reform to the gradual way. The constant and stable function of institutional changes accompanying the gradual reform could be easily accepted and recognized by various interest groups. However, the gradual institutional changes were not for free, but sometimes came at great cost. As discussed previously, financial subsidies incorporated the large quantity of financial resources subject to inefficient allocation. According to the statistics of the World Bank (1996b), in 1994, state-owned enterprises took up 73.5% of total industrial investment but produced 34% of total outputs, and the capital usage for each unit of output of state-owned industrial enterprises was more than twice that of non-state-owned industrial enterprises (page 15). The current performance of gradual reform in China is achieved at the cost of the inefficient allocation of financial resources. It is imaginable that if the condition continues and the out-system outputs cannot grow rapidly and replace the in-system outputs as the major contributor to economic growth, the continuity of the function of institutional changes can hardly be sustained. This is simply because it is impossible to maintain the financial subsidies for a long period due to the large increase of bad debts of state-owned banks corresponding to financial subsidies and rapid accumulation of financial risks.

Fortunately, out-system outputs have realized a rapid growth during the reform. As listed in Table 5.1, the proportion of out-system industrial output value in the

Table 5.1 Proportions of in-system and out-system industrial outputs: 1978–1996

	(%)			
	In-system	*Out-system*	*Out-system I (collective enterprises)*	*Out-system II ("liberalized" enterprises)*
1978	77.63	22.37	22.37	
1979	78.47	21.53	21.53	
1980	75.97	24.03	23.54	0.49
1981	74.78	25.22	24.61	0.61
1982	74.46	25.54	24.82	0.72
1983	73.36	26.64	25.74	0.90
1984	69.08	30.92	29.71	1.21
1985	64.86	35.14	32.08	3.06
1986	62.26	37.74	33.52	4.22
1987	59.73	40.27	34.62	5.65
1988	56.81	43.19	36.14	7.05
1989	56.06	43.94	35.69	8.25
1990	54.60	45.40	35.63	9.77
1991	52.94	47.06	35.70	11.36
1992	48.09	51.91	38.04	13.87

(Continued)

Table 5.1 (Continued)

	(%)			
	In-system	*Out-system*	*Out-system I (collective enterprises)*	*Out-system II ("liberalized" enterprises)*
1993	43.13	56.87	38.36	18.51
1994	40.80	59.20	38.80	20.40
1995	33.97	66.03	36.59	29.44
1996	31.00	69.00	35.00	34.00

Data source and note: Data in this table are calculated based on Table 12 of the *Report on Reform and Development of China 1992–1993: New Breakthroughs and New Challenges*, Table 12 of *Report on Reform and Development of China 1978–1994: The Road of China* and Table 26 of the World Bank (1997). The data of 1996 are estimated by the author.

gross industrial output value rose from 22.37% in 1978 to 69% in 1996, which relieved the social pressure on the state to sustain the growth of in-system outputs to a large extent. In particular, along with the rise of proportion of out-system outputs, the risk in decrease of the proportion of in-system outputs declined correspondingly.

II   The structure of out-system growth and its financial arrangement

Here further attention is paid to the question of how the out-system outputs in China acquired growth. To be specific, while most financial resources were controlled by the state and allocated to the state-owned economy, what did the out-system outputs rely on for growth? If the growth of out-system outputs also depended on certain financial support, then how was the support obtained against the state control?

Many domestic and foreign economists have conducted profound and wide discussions on the cause for the growth of the non-state-owned economy (out-system outputs) and provided many valuable perspectives, such as Nee (1992), Naughton (1994), Li Daokui (1995) and Zhang Jun (1997a), among others. However, most of these articles failed to include the financial arrangement behind the growth of the non-state-owned sector. During the reform, the non-state-owned economy needed to keep a rapid growth rate and was established on a very special structure of capital investment, as it did not compete with the state-owned economy urgently demanding financial support on financial resources.

As proven, the non-state-owned economic outputs, represented by emerging rural enterprises, have realized rapid growth without competing with the state-owned economy on financial resources. According to Table 2.1, despite the rapid rise of the proportion of out-system outputs between 1985 and 1996, the financial support (loans) acquired by the out-system economy only occupied 19.03%

of total loans on average in this period. Theoretically, the growth of economic outputs mainly depends on labor investment and capital investment (as well as technology investment), while the capital investment is divided into external financing and internal financing. The small proportion of (external) financial support obtained by the non-state-owned economy suggested that it mainly relied on internal financing. More importantly, as the capital investment would be very limited at the early stage of development of the non-state-owned economy (which complied with practical conditions), it can be deduced that the out-system economy depends on labor support more because labor support can be acquired more easily for the non-state-owned economy (particularly rural enterprises) and the cost is lower. Then, the rational conclusion is that the non-state-owned economic outputs chose the labor-intensive investment structure since the very beginning, which required relatively less capital that could be generally solved through self-financing. Or, the internal financing exactly matched the less-capital demand of this investment structure. In this way, the out-system economy only showed a limited demand on external financial support. As the labor and land (land for production) investment in the special investment structure of the non-state-owned outputs enjoyed quite favorable costs, the average cost of out-system outputs was far lower than the state-owned economy. In addition, internal financing saved the cost of interest for fund use. As a result, the out-system outputs gained the competitive advantage in the market, thus providing incentives for expansion of production and quick growth of outputs. In this case, the demand on external finance was further reduced and internal finance was strengthened. Moreover, the process of monetization and growth of deposits (money demand) promoted by the out-system outputs conversely helped the financing for the out-system sector and rendered convenient financing for the huge demand of the state-owned economy on financial subsidies.

Nevertheless, this was only the initial condition. Since increasing out-system enterprises poured in the market after seeing the initial development of the non-state-owned economy, the original production function and investment structure of out-system enterprises faced growing pressure. Theoretically, a large number of enterprises of the same category entering the out-system market practically increased the production cost, raising the curve of the marginal cost of out-system enterprises. Under these circumstances, it was necessary to improve the technological content of the production process and upgrade and update products to obtain the higher marginal revenue, that is, wining consumers and market shares with the new design and process. However, improving the technological content naturally required the higher technical standard of the human (labor) capital and, more importantly, the increase of capital investment, particularly the investment of financial resources, which could not be solved merely relying on internal financing. The only way to acquire external financing under the financial arrangement of state monopoly was to obtain credit support by state-owned finance, and the only choice to obtain credit support by state-owned finance was to realize the system coordination and risk guarantee recognized by the state-owned financial system. In this case, the local (rural) governments were involved. As a matter of fact, local governments had already been involved at the initial establishment of most non-state-owned enter-prises, since essential factors to business operation (land, labor and capital) were provided by the government (Chen Jianbo, 1995). The government undertook the task as it had the responsibility and incentive to create jobs and increase incomes.[5] Therefore, the government also had the incentive and responsibility to provide guarantee and seek financial support for rural enterprises. On this basis, the internal financing mentioned prior incorporated the investment by local governments. Local governments could have rendered necessary credit support through the method of guarantee upon the establishment of out-system enterprises. There is reason to believe that the household sector, enterprise sector and local government sector were facing the same utility function in terms of the growth of outputs of non-state-owned enterprises, so it matched the interest goal of local governments to seek financial support for out-system enterprises.

The action of local governments in seeking financial support for out-system enterprises undoubtedly promoted the rapid growth of out-system outputs, but here we are more interested in the changes to the overall financial institutional arrange-ment on the condition of local governments seeking financial support. Beyond any doubt, financial support by local governments would lead to great changes to the investment structure of out-system enterprise; that is, "As it became easier to acquire more cheap capital from the government and banks, enterprises would choose more capital-intensive technologies and constantly expand the investment based on the cheap capital obtained from transactions with the government" (Chen Jianbo, 1995). Then, the out-system outputs and financial support by local govern-ments would form a relation of rigid dependency to some extent. Here the negative effects incurred by this relation are ignored, and the only concern is its influence on the local state-owned financial institutional structure. Apparently, local govern-ments were competing with the state on the right to use financial resources by seeking financial support. The competition constituted an important cause for the former rapid expansion of state-owned financial organizations in space. In other words, under the financial property right framework of state monopoly, the com-petition drove local governments to require setting up branches of state-owned financial organizations, in order to bring convenience to seeking financial support. Meanwhile, it increased the cost of state control on finance. More significantly, the growing demand of out-system outputs on financial support (external financing) boosted the growth of (or generated) the out-system financial institutional factors. Financial support from state-owned finance was limited after all. For instance, among the loans from state-owned banks in 1985, 1990 and 1995, non-state-owned industrial enterprises only accounted for 5.44%, 5.48% and 2.79% (*China Statisti-cal Yearbook*, 1996). Under these circumstances, it was particularly urgent for local governments (as the major protector and supporter of out-system enterprises) to set up their out-system financial system. Seen from the previous financial reform, the out-system financial system consisted of regional commercial banks and cooperative banks supported by local governments, as well as varieties of informal financial departments set up upon the support of the government or emerging spontaneously at a grass-roots level. The emergence of these out-system financial institutional arrangements (or financial property right forms) shows the special significance for the changes of the financial institutional structure of China. Furthermore, the out-system outputs (particularly the out-system outputs II listed in Table 5.1) preferred the small-scale financial service due to their investment structure and small-scale effect. As the facts showed, state-owned financial organizations needed to pay extra costs on credit rating and supervision for the demand of the out-system sector on small-scale financing. It was logical for state-owned financial organizations to establish connections with the capital-intensive large-scale credit demand, while out-system outputs matched the non-government financial system better. The expansion of the out-system financial system would undoubtedly exert competitive pressure on the in-system financial arrangement, so the state always showed an inclination to inhibit the expansion of the out-system financial system. But since the development of the non-state-owned economy constantly generated the demand on this kind of financial system, the out-system finance would always emerge and exist as a kind of institutional supply. The key of the issue lay in that the credit supply rendered by the in-system financial system was far from meeting the financial demand of out-system outputs. As proved by case studies of Zhang Jun (1997b) and Shi Jinchuan et al. (1997), financial support to out-system outputs (particularly the out-system outputs II) basically came from the non-government financial sector (both formal and informal) instead of the regular official financial sector. In view of international experiences, the governments failed to attain the expected result by introducing the regular financial system to provide cheap loans to people in rural areas of many countries in the four decades before 1998. The World Bank (1989b) believed that the formal financial arrangement was often incapable of completely satisfying the requirements of non-corporate sectors. Their financial demand may have been too small in size to formal financial organizations, since the cost of loans or the cost of accepting a deposit was irrelevant to the amount of the transaction. The cost of formal financial organizations on setting up branches in rural area or small towns did not fit their businesses in most cases (page 112). At the same time, the non-governmental informal financial system still existed and developed. In terms of changes to the financial institutional structure, only the financial institutional arrangement born inside the non-state-owned economy was significant, as the real factors contributing to financial growth of the agricultural sector were found in the economic flow of the sector (Zhang Jie, 1995b, page 148). The research of Shi Jinchuan et al. (1997) further demonstrated that the formal non-government financial organizations (such as urban and rural credit cooperatives) were more suitable for the financial demand driven by the growth of out-system outputs than the state-owned financial system.[6] The informal rural financial organizations emerging in China in the 1980s made use of their institutional advantage in civil use and civil management, connected villagers' deposits and borrowings and effectively supervised the loans. By providing farmers with opportunities for small loans at a low transaction cost and guaranteeing recovery of loans for the organizations, the informal rural financial organizations made up the correct solution to the long-term difficulty bothering the formal financial organizations. This solution might be another major institutional innovation in the rural grass-roots society following the rural production responsibility system (Zhu Ling, 1995).

Generally speaking, despite the financial restraint, the out-system outputs have relied on endogenous growth to acquire the financial support rendered by the corresponding out-system financial arrangement. It is worthy to sum up the process of changes to the financial system. It is inappropriate to excessively accuse the state-owned financial system of preference for providing financial support to in-system outputs because the financial support by the state-owned financial system played a key role in the growth of in-system outputs. It is impossible to pay much attention to the non-state-owned outputs. Due to the impossibility of acquiring financial support from the state-owned financial institutional arrangement, the capital structure of "internal financing and support by non-government credits" of out-system enterprises was reinforced, which was favorable to preventing out-system financial dependency. It shall be noted that although the out-system outputs mainly relied on the growth of self-financing and non-bank credits in general, as pointed out by Xiao Geng (1995), a large quantity of funds had been flown to rural enterprises through various channels against the will of the central government. According to statistics, the legal flow of the funds of state-owned banks to rural enterprises accounted for only 2.2% of total loans of state-owned banks in 1979, compared to 6.1% in 1984 and 8.5% in 1991. In addition, among the illegal flow, the shares of rural enterprises in all fixed capital and liquid capital had seen a constant rise from 4.3% in 1979 to 27.5% in 1990; by comparison, the proportion of state-owned enterprises in fixed capital only increased from 5.7% in 1979 to 14.3% in 1990. The so-called illegal capital consisted of funds of state-owned banks from non-banking financial organizations closely associated with state-owned banks (can be considered as the loss of financial subsidies). However, this situation did not affect the efficiency of financial restraint by the state in general.

As proved by experiences in China, the in-system outputs realized constant growth based on the financial restraint and financial support, while the out-system outputs also achieved a high growth rate upon the corresponding financial support from the out-system financial arrangement. What makes more sense is that the emergence of the out-system financial arrangement, being a brand new financial property right form, offered a challenge to the financial property right form of state monopoly. As we can imagine, competition among diversified financial property right forms will show up after rapid expansion of the new financial property right form. We always emphasize that the competition among diversified financial property right forms constitutes the key to financial institutional changes.

4   Ternary theory of finance

I   *Financial dualism of Ronald Mckinnon*

The two financial arrangements and the performance of the growth of outputs during the transition of China have rendered compelling evidence to the financial dualism of Ronald Mckinnon (1996). As mentioned prior, Ronald

Mckinnon is one of the pioneers of the theory of financial deepening. He emphasized the significance of the equilibrium level of the practical interest rate of deposits $(d - p^*)$ to savings mobilization and financial deepening in the initial M-S model mentioned earlier and advocated the reform of financial liberalization that focused on relaxing the control over the interest rate. However, surprisingly, after turning the research perspective to countries with transitional economies, Ronald Mckinnon made a great deal of corrections to these opinions (although he still holds that his current idea shows no difference to his previous ideas in terms of the theoretical standpoint), where he stressed financial control instead of the previous financial liberalization. He believed that although the ideology had been developing towards market liberalism since the 1980s and 1990s, most countries with highly centralized economies suffered a dissatisfying transition because they failed to appropriately apply the internal fiscal control and monetary financial control to guarantee the abdication of interventionism (1996, page 3). China was an exception. In addition to the "Mystery of China" mentioned in Chapter 2, Ronald Mckinnon (1996) also attempted to summarize the special transitional financial arrangement during the successful economic transition with financial dualism. Regarding the special financial arrangement, on one hand, a socialist country that developed based on a highly centralized but "passive" state-owned banking system should consolidate the money and credit system with vigorous action (the financial control and financial restraint by the state as discussed previously) at the initial stage of liberalization; on the other hand, non-centralized enterprises in agriculture and industry should better rely on self-financed funds[7] and borrowings from non-monetary financial resources (the financial arrangement for the growth of out-system outputs mentioned prior in this chapter) before financial conditions become stable.

Financial dualism helped us understand the economic growth and financial arrangement during the transition of China. As pointed out already, the secret to economic growth during the transition of China lay in that China not only assured effective control over state-owned finance to provide sufficient financial subsidies or financial support to in-system outputs, but also enabled the growth of the out-system economy without affecting this financial support (i.e., without leading to loss of subsidies). As facts showed, non-government finance (formal and informal) played an increasingly significant role when out-system outputs of China successfully made use of self-financed funds and acquired the support of financial resources from the non-banking private capital market. Although some out-system outputs (mainly the out-system outputs I) acquired credit support from state-owned banks due to intervention by local governments, the support was limited. For instance, loans from formal financial organizations acquired by all out-system economies including urban collective, private and foreign-funded enterprises and rural enterprises (including agriculture) accounted for less than 20% of total loans in most years between 1985 and 1996. Upon intervention by local governments, rural credit cooperatives provided some loans to collective agricultural organizations and rural enterprises, but the amounts of loans provided to individual farmers were small at the early stage of the reform, and only 10% to 25% of rural residents could acquire loans from cooperatives (Ronald Mckinnon, 1996, page 200). Therefore, the out-system outputs of China strictly followed the financial arrangement of self-financed funds and borrowings from non-monetary financial resources pursuant to the financial dualism. China is a successful example of financial dualism.

II   *Changes to the growth structure during the transition and the ternary transition of the financial arrangement*

The financial dualism of Ronald Mckinnon cannot well explain the financial arrangement for the out-system outputs I (such as rural enterprises) and intervention by local governments, since many rural enterprises had acquired a great quantity of financial support through formal or informal channels based on support by local governments. It also cannot well explain the inclination of local governments to seek credit support to realize economic growth in the area, which objectively boosted economic growth during the transition. Moreover, it cannot explain the logical connection between collective enterprises (out-system I) and emerging liberalized enterprises (out-system II) later. We hereby add one new factor to the financial dualism of Ronald Mckinnon – the growth of outputs upon financial support by local governments. The growth of outputs consists of both in-system (so-called locally administered state-owned enterprises) and out-system (mainly rural enterprises) outputs. We mainly focus on the latter for the convenience of discussion. Then, we can better describe and explain the financial arrangement during the transition of China in a ternary financial framework.

The liberalized enterprises that barely relied on self-financed funds and resources from non-banking capital markets according to Ronald Mckinnon practically referred to the real private enterprises (out-system II), while these enterprises failed to perfectly approach the market during the transition. Compared with rural enterprises, private enterprises might have no local government to help them overcome the access barrier due to the underdeveloped market, while local governments solved many difficulties in rural enterprises' access to the market to a great extent (Naughton, 1994; Nee, 1992). Particularly when the financial market was not open, it was very difficult for private enterprises to acquire funds merely by relying on themselves. In the grey market, it was a very efficient way for many non-state-owned enterprises to involve local governments, since ambiguous property rights protected these enterprises well. Furthermore, privatization (liberalization) was not the best choice of property right institutions in the non-standard economic environment. As the effective market system had not been established and economic liberalization still saw many obstacles during the transition of the economic system, ambiguous property rights arrangements (such as out-system I) were necessary and effective (Tian Guoqiang, 1996; Li Daokui, 1995). It was obviously unrealistic to depend on the growth of liberalized enterprises (out-system II) since the very beginning of the gradual transition.

The out-system I and the corresponding property right arrangement functioned as the intermediate transition, since their market efficiency was lower along with improvements of the market. According to an investigation of the World Bank (1997), 1.5 million collective enterprises which once acted as the driving force for economic growth and employment expansion in China have already seen a decline. In the single year of 1993, they had created approximately 17 million jobs, while the figure was lowered to 14 million after two years. At the same time, private and individual enterprises created 6.6 million jobs. The report of the World Bank concluded that the decline demonstrated the decreasing role of the ambiguous property rights in the growth at the early stage of the reform and suggested that it would no longer boost economic growth. The structure of property rights involving local governments might gradually lower the operation efficiency and flexibility of enterprises, but the non-state-owned enterprises established without participation of the government ushered in opportunities for growth (page 33). This means that the growth of out-system outputs II will become increasingly important after the gradual reform reaches a certain level, and even will become the key to sustain the gradual reform after that time.

In conclusion, the favorable performance of economic growth during the transition in China was apparently derived from the ternary growth structure from top to bottom. In other words, there have been three points to support the growth of the transitional economy and maintain stable economic growth. As shown in Figure 5.5, state-owned, collective and liberalized enterprises all showed great strength like the three legs of a tripod by 1996. Correspondingly, the ternary

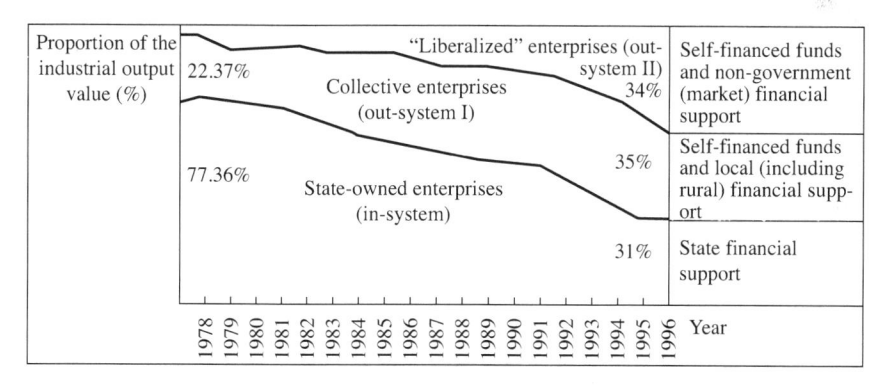

Figure 5.5 Changes to the growth structure during the transition and the ternary financial structure

Data source: Table 5.1 in this book.

transitional pattern for the financial institutional arrangement was formed, which consists of financial control and financial support by the state corresponding to in-system growth, local financial support corresponding to out-system I growth and non-government (market) financial support corresponding to out-system II growth.

Notes

1 According to Table 5.1 in this book, the practical interest rate of deposits of China was negative in 8 years out of the period from 1978 to 1996 and was only −0.165% on average in the 18 years.

2 They separated financial restraint from financial inhibition. The former refers to the concept that the government lowers the interest rate of deposits below the equilibrium interest rate to create the rent for the non-government sector; the latter means that the government lowers the nominal interest rate far below the inflation rate to gain the rent from the non-government sector.

3 Being a structuralist, Joseph Stiglitz had always held an objection to the theory of financial deepening. He once criticized financial liberalization from the perspective of market failure, believed that financial liberalization would lead to market failure and stood for moderate interference by the government. He even stated that the moderate financial inhibition was beneficial and harmless in case of incomplete information (refer to Wang Jizu, 1997). According to his latest research (1997), governments in East Asia have played a positive role in assuring the safe and perfect financial system and creating new institutions and markets to fill the gap of the non-government sector. Therefore, the analysis framework of financial restraint he proposed jointly with others reflects his consistent idea. Financial restraint is considered the condition between financial inhibition and financial liberalization and is regarded as a model more attractive than the other two choices.

4 If the hypothesis of the closed economy is abandoned, capital flight should not be ignored. In this case, in addition to restricting on asset substitution, it is also very important to restrict on capital flight, otherwise it will affect the overall efficiency of restriction on asset substitution. According to a research report made by adviser Wharf from the Royal Institute of International Affairs for OECD, the total amount of capital flight of China between 1989 and 1995 possibly exceeded USD 100 billion, including about USD 50 billion not approved by the government. See more detailed discussions in Wang Jun (1996).

5 Chen Jianbo believed that the goal of rural enterprises in China was no longer the single goal of profit at the neoclassical level, but was a comprehensive goal combining the goal of local governments (communities) to increase incomes, create new jobs and expand fiscal capability and even the goal of individual officials in the government. Due to the underdeveloped market, all factors essential in establishment of enterprises such as labor recruitment, land acquisition and credit capital and even engagements with the administration for industry and commerce or the tax authority were organized by the government based on the governmental power. Moreover, facing an extremely strange external world, new entrepreneurs must rely on protection by the government for survival.

6 According to the cases in Shi Jinchuan et al. (1997), Zhejiang Road & Bridge, a leader among small-sized private enterprises, had only 32.67% of its total deposits and 25.79% of its total loans transacted with the major four state-owned specialized banks, compared to respectively 67.33% and 74.21% with non-government financial organizations (urban and rural credit cooperatives). More significantly, the overdue loan ratio of Road &

Bridge was only 0.612% in the urban credit cooperatives in 1996, while the dead and bad loan ratio was only 0.003% and the capital adequacy ratio reached 8.48%. Based on case studies of Zhang Jun (1997b), in the rural finance market of Wenzhou in 1993, the capital of state-owned banks and cooperatives only occupied 20%, compared to 40% of non-government capital and 40% of self-financed capital.

7 In the opinion of Ronald Mckinnon, self-financed funds could avoid some difficulties. At the initial stage of marketization, liberalized enterprises had no condition to apply for loans to banks, such as the barrier in the credit record or risk guarantee and how to establish a fine corporate structure (1996, page 197).

6 Dilemma of property rights under the state-owned financial system and the path of solution

1 Dilemma of state-owned financial property rights

I Boundary of financial organizations and financial property rights

The state has a strong preference for expanding the boundary of its financial property rights by enlarging the scale of state-owned financial organizations during the gradual reform in China. In essence, expanding the boundary of state-owned financial property rights is to hold the control right over saving resources and perform financial support, thus seeking for constant and stable growth of in-system outputs. Then, why does China only rely on expansion of organizations to expand the boundary of financial property rights? Is there any other way that is more economic and more effective to expand the boundary of financial property rights? Is there a method that does not involve the contraction path after expansion of the boundary of financial property rights? In other words, how can China make the financial property right forms generated through the expansion of the boundary of property rights an element that directly constitutes the new financial institutional structure instead of leaving it as a transitional institutional arrangement?

Apparently, there is no other way better than expanding the boundary of state-owned financial property rights. As stressed several times, under a centrally planned economic system, there is an urgent demand to gather and control the national income (or deposits) exposed to constant decentralization in the reform process through the expansion of a certain financial property right form within a short term, thus seeking compensation of the reform cost and the financial support to in-system outputs. Based on discussions in Chapter 5, the financial property right form of state monopoly enjoys the comparative advantage in mobilizing savings, since it is capable of rapidly providing deposit certificates in a large quantity according to the aggregate principle (i.e., the total cost equal to the total revenue). As the expansion of deposits is a function of the expansion of organizations, the large-scale provision of deposit certificates necessarily requires the large enough scale and rapid enough expansion of financial organizations that supply deposit certificates. In view of this, the comparative advantage of the financial property right form of state monopoly in savings mobilization is manifested by its comparative advantage in the expansion of financial organizations. In this way, the fund sources that cover the reform cost of the state and the demand on financial support are satisfied, when the state has realized the maximum utility and the path of gradual reform has been formed. As revealed in the prior discussions, the expansion of the boundary of state-owned financial property rights mainly depends on the expansion of the boundary of state-owned financial organizations. It is a unique situation in financial institutional changes in China where the boundary of financial property rights is expanded through the expansion of the boundary of organizations or deviation from the market area.

However, it is unrealistic to mobilize savings and apply the funds to serve gradual reform by expanding competitive (such as non-state-owned) financial property right forms since the market environment is not perfect. From the perspective of economics, it can be demonstrated that these property right forms function efficiently in mobilizing savings and allocating financial resources, the financial institutional arrangement formed in the process will grow to be a new financial institutional factor or these financial property right forms will relieve the surplus of financial organizations and reduce the quantity of bad debts. However, based on the initial conditions and the gradual reform path of China, it is logical to have the efficient competitive financial institutional arrangement lag behind the inefficient state-owned financial arrangement. The key may lie in that China cannot wait for the natural generation of an efficient competitive financial system due to the urgent demand on deposit resources during the gradual reform. Practical utility is greatly highlighted when choosing the institutional arrangement during the process of institutional changes. On this basis, the theoretically superior institutional arrangement is often replaced by a more practical, although theoretically inferior, institutional arrangement. The primary issue for the gradual reform is how many financial resources can be applied to financial support" instead of "how to effectively make use of financial resources. Between the two alternatives, the monopolistic financial institutional arrangement and the competitive financial institutional arrangement, the former one that can acquire the most financial resources is chosen during the institutional evolution but not the latter one that can allocate financial resources in the most efficient way. Once the state-owned financial institutional arrangement becomes the leading institutional arrangement for its comparative advantage in mobilizing financial resources, the non-state-owned financial institutional arrangement (with comparative advantage in allocating financial resources) will be excluded or even cut out and will only be listed as an alternative of institutional selection when efficiency in allocation of financial resources is more demanded in the whole process of institutional evolution.

In light of these discussions, the excessive expansion of the boundary of state-owned financial organizations in China complies with the logic of gradual reform, which determines that the contraction of the boundary of state-owned financial organizations shall also follow the logic of gradual reform. Since the expansion of the boundary of state-owned financial property rights is promoted by the expansion of the boundary of organizations, a logical conclusion can be reached that the contraction of the boundary of state-owned financial property rights shall start from the contraction of the boundary of organizations. However, the question is that the whole logical process is irreversible. In other words, the result of expansion of organizations is the expansion of property rights, but the result of contraction of organizations may not be the contraction of property rights. This is because when the boundary of property rights of a certain scale has been formed through expansion of organizations, it will incorporate many more complicated things than the boundary of organizations. To be specific, it consists of not only the right to control financial resources and earn financial returns but also the corresponding obligations, particularly the massive financial risks accumulated over the years resulting from financial subsidies. Despite the fact that the state could abolish and merge state-owned financial organizations in an administrative manner, the financial risks in the boundary of state-owned financial property rights cannot be reduced. The state is able to lower the control cost and improve the control performance by contracting the boundary of organizations but cannot eliminate some social responsibilities borne by state-owned financial organizations.

II   Division of state-owned financial property rights and indispensability of state guarantee

Theoretically, the most direct way to contract the boundary of state-owned financial property rights corresponding to the efficiency of allocation of financial resources and X efficiency is, dividing property rights. This means to rapidly separate state-owned financial property rights[1] and guarantee that each segment of state-owned financial property rights enjoys symmetry between benefit and risk. This method seems very attractive theoretically, but it has to meet harsh conditions before it can be executed. The most striking condition is that the state could hand over financial property rights at one time and would no longer bear the responsibility of final settlement, which means that the state would transfer its property rights on state-owned banks (including the control right, residual claims, risk guarantee obligation etc.) to state-owned banks. The state would abandon direct financial control and financial guarantee. This method can have two results. The first is that the state may hand over property rights without performing recapitalization against state-owned banks. This is no different from advocating bankruptcy of state-owned banks. As discussed, the asset ratio of state-owned banks is very low (only 4.34% in 1996) and is mainly sustained by the household deposits under the state guarantee (control). Once the state advocates withdrawing from the control, it means that the state no longer provides guarantee. In view of the extreme significance of state control to money demand in China (see Chapter 4), this would definitely shake people's willingness in deposits. The requirement on liquidity of deposits and withdrawals cannot be satisfied with the self-owned funds of banks that only take up 5.54% of deposits and the small amount of deposit reserves. The following discussion in this chapter demonstrates that the control and guarantee by the state actually constitutes an important investment for state-owned banks or is considered part of self-owned funds. This is the characteristic of the state-owned financial property right structure in China. Along with the further development of reform, the investment proportion of the state in the form of guarantee is rising every year, and the significance and risk weight of the guarantee is increasing. Based on the guarantee, the household deposits at state-owned banks are stable enough for banks to apply the funds as self-owned funds. If the state-owned financial property rights are divided and the state guarantee is withdrawn, the virtual capital that the state originally contributed in the form of guarantee would disappear, leading to serious imbalance in the state-owned financial capital structure. Therefore, it is apparently impossible to carry out division of property rights based on the logic of gradual reform in China.

For the other result, the state performs recapitalization against state-owned banks when handing over financial property rights, that is, investing real capital to replace the original virtual capital provided in form of guarantee, but the key issue is whether the state can afford the real capital. The cost is not small, as indicated in Table 6.1. According to conservative estimates by the author, the real capital that the state should have invested reached as high as 231.483 billion Yuan in 1996, while the figure should have been between 400 and 500 billion Yuan according to the World Bank. If calculating the net worth, the investment attained 639.420 billion Yuan. Obviously, it is impossible for the state to contribute so much capital to recapitalization of state-owned banks within a short period. Even if the state could pay the cost of recapitalization as a lump sum, the property rights might not be handed over successfully. The prerequisite for these discussions is that state-owned banks basically have no bad debt, but the bad debts have rapidly accumulated at state-owned banks according to the empirical investigation in Chapter 2. For instance, in 1996, the proportion of loans that could not be recovered was 6% based on conservative estimates (accounting for 37.95% of bad debts of the year), and the state had to offer 379.480 billion Yuan to write off the bad debts. However, as suggested in Table 6.1, the scale of write-offs of the state was only 20 billion Yuan in 1996, and the state intended to render a fund of only 140 billion Yuan for write-offs between 1997 and 2000.[2] It shall be noted that the total assets of state-owned banks would decrease and the investment of the state would be correspondingly reduced when the state writes off the bad debts of state-owned banks. Even so, the state still needs to invest a considerable amount of funds. Nevertheless, if the state can afford this cost of recapitalization, it suggests that the state is still capable of maintaining the existing state-owned financial property rights and thus has no incentive (or need) to divide financial property rights and carry out commercialization over state-owned banks.

In view of these discussions, the market-oriented contraction of the boundary of state-owned financial property rights (division of property rights) will face one of the two results, maintaining the existing boundary of property rights or carrying out the radical property rights division, that is, choosing between no action and bankruptcy, with no other choice. However, both results do not comply with the logic of gradual reform in China. If maintaining the current boundary of property rights, the financial risks will continue to accumulate, necessarily leading to the

Table 6.1 State investment in state-owned banks: 1979–1996

	(Billion Yuan)						
	1990	*1991*	*1992*	*1993*	*1994*	*1995*	*1996*
Author's estimation on investment	3.199	16.697	11.892	18.222	99.803	183.949	231.483
The World Bank's estimation on investment	39.906	60.193	85.427	120.084	182.836	–	–
Estimation on investment based on net worth	23.468	66.332	284.813	298.019	409.408	604.051	639.420
Value of bad debts that should be written off	84.189	103.070	121.345	179.230	245.417	308.289	379.480
Value of bad debts that have been written off						2.400	20.000

Data source and note: The data in this table is calculated based on Table 2.5, 2.7, 2.8 and 2.9 of this book. Here we calculate the scale of state investment required to meet the core capital ratio of 8% specified in the *Basel Agreement*. The value of the author's estimation is smaller than the estimation of the World Bank because the latter only incorporates the data of the major four state-owned specialized banks, and the former additionally includes the People's Bank of China and CITIC Industrial Bank. If only based on the data of the major four state-owned specialized banks, the investment scale in 1992 and 1996 would far surpass the author's estimate. Moreover, a great part of the self-owned funds of state-owned banks are virtual capital. The value of bad debts that should be written off is calculated based on 5% of total assets of the year before 1992 and based on 6% between 1993 and 1996, while the two ratios here are determined upon the official announcement on the proportion of bad debts in total loans. The practical ratios may be even higher. The value of bad debts that have been written off refers to Zhang Chunlin (1997).

radical path sooner or later; if the risks are decentralized by property rights division through the market, state-owned financial property rights will be restricted by the indispensability of state guarantee.

III   Reform within the boundary of state-owned financial property rights and dilemma of property rights

When risks start accumulating in large number in the state-owned financial property right arrangement, the spontaneous (also rational) reaction of the state, the contributor, is to prevent externalization of financial risks through stricter financial control instead of decentralizing risks by dividing financial property rights. The division of financial property rights not only signifies the state withdrawing from the guarantee but also suggests the state giving up financial control. The state is aware of the consequences of giving up financial control. Therefore, the division of financial property rights and the two possible results discussed prior do not comply with the utility function of the state and thus will not turn into practical reform. As the state is still exerting powerful control over economic and financial processes, ideas on reform (reform proposals and theories) will only turn into practical reform when they comply with the utility function of the state (Zhang Jie, 1998b). The state abolishing or merging state-owned financial organizations does not mean that the state will abandon its control over state-owned financial organizations. Conversely, the contraction of organizations will only strengthen state control over state-owned financial property rights. No matter how the boundary of state-owned financial organizations is contracted, the original intention of state control can hardly be changed. Since the state is still the contributor, the symmetry between risk and benefit can only be realized when the state controls state-owned financial property rights. Undoubtedly, the state always hopes to change the arrangement of financial property rights and decentralize financial risks without damaging its financial control.

In view of previous experience of financial reform in China, the state has been attempting to adjust the arrangement of financial property rights without changing the boundary of state-owned financial property rights (i.e., without abandoning guarantee and financial control), theoretically known as commercialization of state-owned banks. The state holds a very clear intention to maintain the existing boundary of state-owned financial property rights and meanwhile improve the efficiency of allocation of financial resources and X efficiency, in order to mitigate financial risks and reduce the net cost on financial control by the state. Theoretically, the state would acquire the maximum utility when these attempts succeeded. A logical conclusion can be reached that the state would only make other choices when it finds it impossible to attain the result it expects through these attempts. Only after the state pays enough learning costs and becomes aware that the expected cost will exceed the expected return would it withdraw from these attempts. In this sense, the attempts at commercialization of state-owned banks obviously conform to the state's goal of maximum utility.

The time that the state started the aforementioned attempts exactly matched the turning point described in Chapter 2. As state, the cost of financial control by the state exceeded the return for the first time in 1992, suggesting the rapid accumulation of financial risks since this year. After that, state control over state-owned finance became decreasingly cost-effective, and the expansion of the boundary of state-owned financial property rights that had lasted for 14 years reversed. The state decided to accelerate reform of the financial sector at the end of 1993 as a response to the rapid rise of control costs in 1992. In that year, the state officially proposed the idea of commercialization of state-owned banks and made corresponding attempts. Many institutional changes and financial reforms between 1994 and 1996 laid wires for the execution of the reform ideas. See details in Table 6.2.

In general, institutional preparations over this period strengthened the actual financial control by the state rather than creating conditions for commercialization of state-owned banks. The state largely relied on formal institutional arrangements (such as financial laws and regulations) to weaken the influence of local governments and state-owned banks to achieve the result. Although the state started writing off bad debts in 1994 and established policy banks to take over

Table 6.2 Financial control and reform by the state: 1988–1996

Time	Reform and background
1988–1989	Monetization index declined for the first time. The originally active financial control by the state became passive. Macroeconomic and social political conditions became abnormal.
1990–1991	The state embarked on reducing non-banking financial organizations such as trust and investment companies and finance companies.
1992	The cost of financial control by the state exceeded the return for the first time.
1993	The state accelerated reform of the financial sector, mainly implementing commercialization reform of state-owned banks and strengthening financial control by the state.
1994	The *Budget Law* was approved by the National People's Congress, which prohibited the government from borrowing from the central bank. Three policy banks were established. Since this year, the bad debts were written off in pilot banks. This was the first-stage preparation for commercialization of state-owned banks.
1995	The *Law of the People's Republic of China on the People's Bank of China* and the *Law of the People's Republic of China on Commercial Banks* were approved by the National People's Congress. The former prohibited overdraft and direct loans from the People's Bank of China to the central and provincial governments, while the latter required state-owned banks to hold capital equal to 8% of total assets exposed to risk adjustments, and meanwhile to improve the management on asset-liability ratio through appropriate plans. Meanwhile, the *Insurance Law*, *Negotiable Instruments Law* and *Guarantee Law* were approved, which were powerful measures to strengthen financial control as well as institutional preparation for the second stage of commercialization of state-owned banks.
1996	The national interbank lending market was established and control on the interbank lending interest rate was relaxed in a limited way. Ownerships between state-owned banks and non-banking financial organizations were terminated. Since April 1, the open market businesses started. This was the third-stage institutional preparation for commercialization of state-owned banks.

part of policy-related loans from state-owned banks, no evidence suggests the reduction of policy-related loans rendered by state-owned banks or re-loans by the central bank (Xiao Geng, 1997, page 347). It can be seen that the state had little room to choose between strengthening financial control and commercializing state-owned banks, and the state could not combine the two goals of reform together. More profoundly, this was because the two goals contradicted each other. To be specific, if any progress is made in commercialization of state-owned banks within the framework of state-owned financial property rights, it means that financial control by the state is weakened. The core of commercialization of state-owned banks lies in capital autonomy. If state-owned banks are endowed with capital autonomy when state-owned financial property rights are maintained, it will undoubtedly lead to the rising influence of local preference and preference of state-owned banks and the declining influence of state preference. Consequently, the state will lose control over finance. As a contributor, the state will not allow local preference and preference of state-owned banks above its own preference, so it will spontaneously reduce and even eliminate these preferences, which implies the loss of capital autonomy of state-owned banks. Then the state-owned banks have no power to independently use these funds, not to mention commercialized operation. As proved by facts, financial control by the state was strengthened between 1993 and 1996, and no progress had been made in commercialization of state-owned banks.

We can see that the reform of the state-owned financial system is facing a dilemma of property rights. Theoretically, the prerequisite for commercialization of state-owned banks is to divide state-owned financial property rights and make state-owned banks a new type of financial organization with internalized benefits and risks. As demonstrated by previous discussions, the division of state-owned financial property rights was completely unfeasible. Based on the existing boundary of state-owned financial property rights, it is logical to choose financial monopoly (centralization) instead of commercialization (decentralization). As mentioned, the state-owned banks are endowed with credit autonomy through commercialization, stimulating state-owned banks to allocate financial resources pursuant to their preferences. Since state-owned financial property rights cannot be divided, so-called commercialization only realized fragmentary financial property rights of state-owned banks. In particular, the state would continue to provide guarantee if state-owned financial property rights are not divided, so state-owned banks that acquire a part of property rights will not bear final responsibilities for credits and will necessarily conduct opportunistic behaviors to pursue the maximum utility. Then, the state will re-strengthen its control over state-owned banks to make credits of state-owned banks comply with state preference (such as financial support). To sum up, once the boundary of state-owned financial property rights still exists, financial control by the state will be necessary and rational no matter how low the allocation efficiency and X efficiency are. Under these circumstances, commercialization of state-owned banks that was advocated by the state will finally fail. Even if commercialization was initiated, state control will return after a period. This situation is also manifested by the frequent periodic rectification of the financial order.

Fundamentally, the arrangement of state-owned financial property rights and direct control over state-owned banks by the state cannot and shall not be separated. It is an unalterable principle that the state has its financial organizations serve its maximum utility, just as private financial organizations serving the maximum interests of their contributors. Complaints on the too little capital autonomy of state-owned banks given by the state and too heavy taxes and interests are actually nonsense. As they are owned by the state, why must the state transfer the autonomy, and why can't the state collect more taxes and interests? Moreover, the low efficiency of state-owned banks is not a simple question. From the perspective of the state, it is the greatest efficiency that state-owned banks supply considerable financial support and guarantee the success of gradual reform. It is actually the duty of state-owned banks to pursue this efficiency. A truth implied in our discussions is that if state-owned banks prematurely pursue their efficiency in resource allocation, not enough financial support can be provided to the gradual reform of China. The inefficient use of funds (in a neoclassical sense) of state-owned banks practically promoted the stable growth of in-system outputs and avoided the J-shaped decline that took place in the Soviet Union and Eastern Europe. As pointed out in Section 1, Point 1 of this chapter, the gradual reform of China first requires the scale of allocation of financial resources and then pursues the efficiency of allocation, while the state-owned financial system exactly satisfies the requirements. Even after China begins to pursue efficiency in allocation of financial resources as we assume, the requirement on efficiency of state-owned banks will still be special. Where state-owned financial property rights cannot be divided, the efficiency of state-owned banks cannot be measured by efficiency in resource allocation or the returns of banks, but shall be decided by the scale of financial resources allocated by state-owned banks. To be more specific, when economic reform exerts a lower requirement on the scale of allocation of financial resources but a higher requirement on the efficiency of allocation of financial resources, the scale of financial resources allocated by state-owned banks shall be reduced. The reduction itself constitutes a contribution to the overall efficiency in allocation of financial resources. As the reform is deepening, the state-owned financial system seems more inefficient, not because it is monopolized by the government or owned by the state but because its relative scale is expanding. Therefore, the monopolistic status of government over state-owned banks shall be strengthened rather than weakened during the reform. The monopoly by state-owned banks only becomes an issue when the economy still lacks a commercial financial system of a large relative scale (Zhang Jie, 1997b). It is essential to recognize this point for correctly understanding the changes of the state-owned financial system in China and finding the solution to the dilemma of property rights.

2   The model of bad debts of state-owned banks

I   Bad debts and gradual transition

Under normal conditions, bad debts of banks indicate the low efficiency of banks in allocation of financial resources. A large number of bad debts may be accumulated due to limited financial information, mistakes in credits decisions, inadequate supervision and management of banks and so on. These bad debts can be reduced and inhibited through the efforts and technical improvements of banks and meanwhile can be written off with bad debts reserves. Moreover, during the process that banks are competing to prevent and clear bad debts, one can obviously see the emerging financial innovation, changes to the financial institutional structure and the consequent improvement of efficiency of financial resource allocation (Zhang

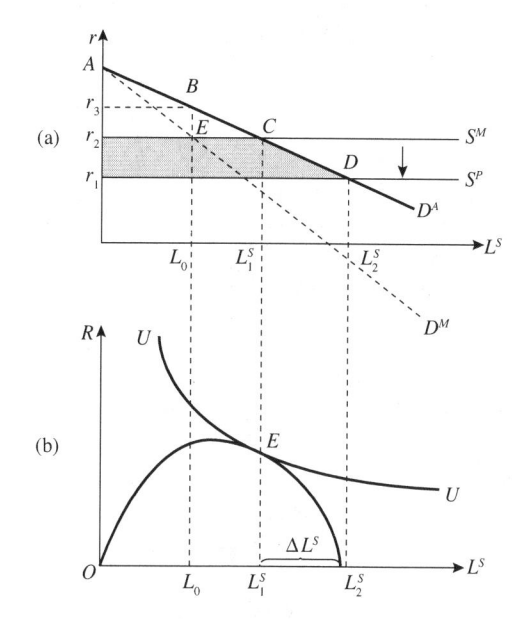

Figure 6.1 Bad debts and financial support

Jie, 1997b). However, the bad debts of state-owned banks in China shall not be entirely linked up with the mistakes of banks or simply deemed as manifestations of low efficiency in allocation of financial resources. In fact, the bad debts of state-owned banks in China are directly related to the gradual transition.

It is necessary to establish an explanatory model that meets mainstream economic norms, in order to assure the theoretical generality of the bad debts of state-owned banks. This model is intuitively illustrated with Figure 6.1. In Figure 6.1, Figure 6.1 (a) is built on a standard firm equilibrium model, while Figure 6.1 (b) is directly copied from Figure 3.5. First, let's look at Figure 6.1 (a). The horizontal axis L^S indicates the scale of loans. The vertical axis r means the capital price (interest rate). Line D^A refers to the average credit demand, which shows an inverse function relationship with the interest rate by downward sloping to the right. D^M is the line of marginal credit demand, generally under D^A. S^M and S^P respectively represent the market supply and planned supply of credits. Three cases deserve attention here. In the first case, if the state-owned bank operates based on commercial principles and is facing a competitive financial (credit) market, it will provide credits with the interest rate of r_2 following the line S^M, and the quantity of credits provision is L^S_1. In the second case, if the state-owned bank operates based on commercial principles but is facing a monopolistic credit market, it will provide credits pursuant to the principle of $D^M = S^M$, that is, providing credits in a smaller scale (L_0) at a higher monopoly price (r_3). In the third case, there is no complete credit market, and the state-owned bank allocates credits according to the government's preferences to provide financial support to the transitional economy instead of operating based on commercial principles. In this case, the state-owned bank will provide cheap credits at a larger scale (L^S_2) at a lower planned price (r_1) following the line S^P.

Furthermore, the performances of state-owned banks in providing credits are completely different in these three cases. In the first case, in the competitive credit market, state-owned banks can only provide credits with the market equilibrium interest rate r_2, and other financial organizations joining the credit market jointly share average revenue, so state-owned banks are exposed to zero credit surplus. According to modern microeconomics, the status of zero credit surplus best reflects the market competition and efficiency in allocation of financial resources. In the second case, the state-owned banks hold the monopoly position and enjoy a positive credit surplus based on the monopoly price. In Figure 6.1 (a), the credit surplus brought by the monopoly is represented by the area of BEr_2r_3 (i.e., the part where the practical price of credit exceeds the supply of market credits). Under this situation, society also suffers the net loss represented by the area of triangle BEC due to the monopoly finance (i.e., the so-called Harberger triangle area), but state-owned banks themselves have acquired extra credit surpluses. In terms of the credit surplus in the third case, since the state-owned banks provide credits at the lower planned price r_1 (lower than the market equilibrium price planned price r_2), the credit surplus will be necessarily negative. The negative credit surplus is reflected by the part where the line of planned supply of credits S^P is lower than the market supply of credits S^M and is represented by area r_2CDr_1 of the shaded trapezium in Figure 6.1 (a).

It shall also be noted that it is theoretically extremely imprecise that the domestic theoretical realm considers the state-owned banking system in China as a monopolistic institutional arrangement. In view of these three cases, the institutional arrangement of state-owned banks of China is far different from the monopoly financial arrangement in a strict sense. If it was monopolistic, it should have allocated resources with a higher price and a smaller scale. However, as a matter of fact, it allocated resources in an opposite way. It is more accurate to describe the financial institutional (market) structure of China where state-owned banks dominate with the concept of financial restraint or financial repression. In this sense, it is correct for Ronald Mckinnon and Edward Shaw to regard the rise of the credit price of banks (or liberalization of the interest rate) as the core step when they proposed the theory of financial repression or financial deepening. Only through this step can these banks reduce their negative credit surpluses and have the capability and incentives to enter the credit market and allocate resources. Nevertheless, as the word is widely accepted through common practices, this book also uses the word "monopoly" often when discussing state-owned finance. Readers should pay attention to identify the true meaning of "monopoly" when the word is mentioned in this book.

Apparently, the state-owned banks of China allocate credits during the transition through the method described in the third case. The reason has been detailed in previous chapters (particularly Chapters 3 and 4). It shall be pointed out that in the first and second cases, in-system outputs in the transitional economy cannot acquire sufficient financial support. As seen from Figure 6.1 (b), the credit supplies in the two cases are respectively L_0 and L^S_{1}. With the larger L^S_{1} as an example, it has a gap of ΔL^s compared to L^S_{2}, the credit quantity demanded during the gradual transition. The gap can only be covered in the third case. Therefore, state-owned banks pay the cost of negative credit surplus thus to provide sufficient credit support to in-system outputs during the transition. In other words, state-owned finance bought the gradual transition at a price of the negative credit surplus, which further proves the proposition proposed in Chapter 3. The negative credit surplus also suggests that the state has transferred a part of the credit surplus of state-owned banks, equal to the area of the shaded trapezium, to state-owned enterprises through the special institutional arrangement. As a result, in-system outputs have seen stable growth and the gradual reform has been successfully implemented, while a large quantity of bad debts have accumulated in the book of state-owned banks and a large amount of virtual capital has shown up in the capital structure of state-owned banks. Thus, the area of the shaded trapezium in Figure 6.1 (a) is the limit for the operating loss of state-owned banks, and the ΔL^s in Figure 6.1 (b) equals the theoretical scale of bad debts.

Also according to these discussions, before other financial property right forms develop to be a competitive credit market and when state-owned banks still hold a share of over 75% in the credit market, if state-owned banks completely comply with commercial principles in operation (the practical feasibility is not considered here), the situation of the first case will appear. This is a disastrous result for a transitional economy. When in-system enterprises fail (practically they are incapable) to get enough credit support and the state does not render fiscal support, the economy would suffer from J-shaped decline. This also demonstrates that it is unfeasible to unilaterally implement commercialization during the gradual reform when state-owned banks hold the monopoly status, since it contradicts the logic of gradual reform.

II   The credit equilibrium model of state-owned banks

According to previous economic literature, economists have put forward three different credit equilibrium models. The first is the neoclassical credit equilibrium model, as shown in Figure 6.2. This model consists of a line of credit supply slanting upward and a line of credit demand sloping downward, while the credit equilibrium is decided by the intersect of the two lines, E. The equilibrium credit supply is L^* and the credit supply price (interest rate) is represented by r^*. The interest rate automatically adjusts the supply and demand of credits. For example, when the interest rate is the lower r_{1}, the excessive credit demand ΔD will show up: $D(r_{1}) > S(r_{1})$. Then r will move upward, until $r_{1} \rightarrow r^*$ and $S(r^*) = D(r^*)$. When the interest rate is the higher r_{2}, the excessive credit supply ΔS will show up: $S(r_{2}) > D(r_{2})$. Then r will move downward, until $r_{2} \rightarrow r^*$ and $S(r^*) = D(r^*)$.

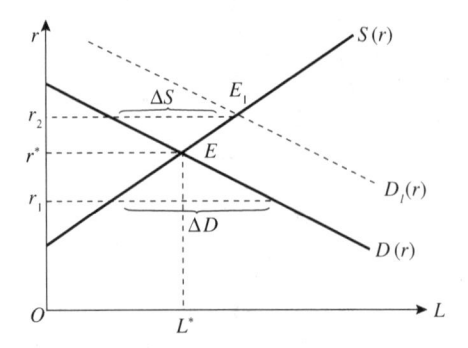

Figure 6.2 Neoclassical credit equilibrium model

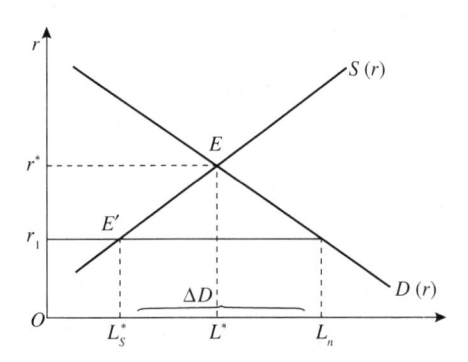

Figure 6.3 Government-intervention credit equilibrium model

The second is the government-intervention credit equilibrium model, a kind of non-Walrasian credit equilibrium model. To carry out certain credit preferential policy, the government artificially depressed the upper limit of the interest rate to a lower level, thus making the credit demand greater than the credit supply. Since the interest rate is determined by the government and fixed, it no longer plays a role in automatically adjusting the supply and demand of credits. As shown in Figure 6.3, despite the excessive credit demand of ΔD, the bank can only provide the credits of L_s*. In this case, E' is a credit equilibrium deviated from Walrasian equilibrium. Only a part of credit demands (based on government preference) are satisfied. This model features two key assumptions. First, all practical credit demands $D(r)$ are rational without low X efficiency in allocation of financial resources and rigid credit demand, or, in other words, the credit demand is very sensitive to r. Once the control over the upper limit of the interest rate is relaxed, it will no longer stay at L_D but will automatically approach L*. Second, no financial institution other than the banking system controlled by the government provides credits. In other words, the government is exerting complete control over credits, and the banking system under the government control does not conduct any opportunistic behavior.

The third is the credit rationing equilibrium model. This model, created by Stiglitz and Weiss (1981), is attained by relaxing the hypothesis of complete information of the neoclassical credit equilibrium model. They believed that even without government intervention, credit rationing could be a long-term equilibrium since borrowers might be exposed to adverse selection and moral risks.[3] As a matter of fact, if the lender has complete information, credit rationing will not emerge, because the lender could collect a higher interest rate based on different possibilities of repayment and provide loans to all applicants who are willing to pay the appropriate interest rate. Therefore, the root cause for credit rationing is lack of information. No matter how prudent the lender is, there must be some information missing (Stiglitz, 1993, page 554). The credit rationing equilibrium model is a correction to the neoclassical credit equilibrium model considering the incomplete information.

Figure 6.4 reveals the credit rationing equilibrium. *D(r)*, the curve of credit demand, in the first quadrant shows no change compared with Figure 6.2, but the curve of credit supply, originally linear, becomes nonlinear. This change takes place after the information factor is considered. It means that in case of complete information, the curve of credit supply bending backward in Figure 6.4 will be restored to be the straight line in Figure 6.2. For the nonlinear variation of the curve of credit supply, the credit supply upon the equilibrium interest rate *(r*)* changes from the original L^* to current L_R^*, indicating that the credit demands of $\Delta\bar{D}$ cannot be satisfied. These credit demands that cannot be satisfied consist of both disqualified credit demands and demands of qualified borrowers. Therefore, the root cause still lies in that the lender cannot tell the qualified from the disqualified in $\Delta\bar{D}$ due to incomplete information.

The curve of credit supply bends backward mainly for the following reason. In the neoclassical credit equilibrium model, the quantity of credits supplied by the lender is decided by the interest rate (the interest rate is also decided by the

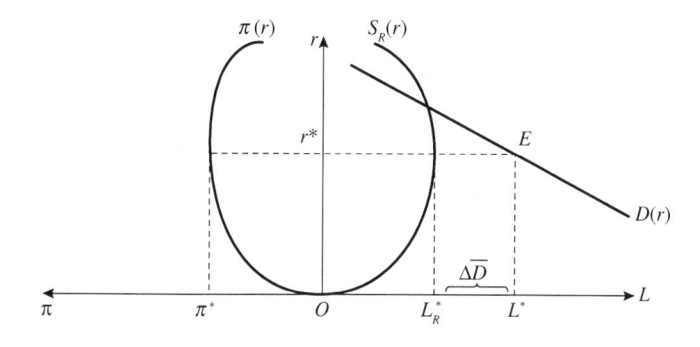

Figure 6.4 Credit rationing equilibrium model

quantity of credit demand). If the borrower accepts the high price, such as r_2 in Figure 6.2, the lender can provide more credits (such as ΔS) at the price until the new credit equilibrium is reached, such as E_1, the intersect of $DI(r)$ and $S(r)$ in Figure 6.2. However, in the credit rationing equilibrium model, the quantity of credits provided by the lender is decided by the average return of credits in addition to the price of the loan. The concern is that the loan price *(r)* and the average return of credits *(π)* do not fit each other perfectly. In the second quadrant of Figure 6.4, one can see that the average return of credits *(π)* increases with the rise of the interest rate of the loan at the beginning, but after the interest rate of the loan reaches *(r*)* and π grows to the maximum *(π*)*, the average return of credits drops when the interest rate of the loan further increases. At this time, the lender will not increase the supply of loans no matter how high an interest rate the borrower pays (or is willing to pay). In general, optimum borrowers will give up borrowing in cases of high interest rate, when only those who are willing to take great risks will continue to apply for borrowings. The banks are concerned about the high possibility of risk-taking behaviors and the high credit risks at the high interest rate. As a result, the increase of interest rate may lower instead of increase the expected revenue of the bank. Therefore, banks are willing to reject a part of loan applications at the relatively low interest rate but are not willing to approve all borrowers' applications at the high interest rate (Stiglitz, 1993, pages 554–555; Zhang Weiying, 1996, page 563). As manifested in Figure 6.4, the curve of credit supply bends after the interest rate reaches r*.

Although these credit equilibrium models cannot independently explain the credit equilibrium of state-owned banks in China, they help us build the new explanatory model. Here we will re-explain these credit equilibrium models based on the conditions in China and create the credit equilibrium model of state-owned banks in China on this basis.

First, let's observe the neoclassical credit equilibrium model and the credit rationing equilibrium model. As is known to us, the only difference between the two models is the existence of the information factor. As the neoclassical credit equilibrium model is built upon the hypothesis of complete information, the interest rate becomes the only factor that decides the credit provision of the bank. Only if the credit demand side holds a strong enough demand on credits and accepts a high interest rate will the credit equilibrium be realized at the high interest rate (such as point E_1 in Figure 6.2, where the interest rate is the higher r_2). In the credit rationing model, the quantity of credits provided by banks is directly determined by the average return of credits instead of the interest rate. Considering the information cost and credit risk, the high interest rate is often accompanied by high credit risk and thus lowers the average return of credits. Therefore, credit equilibrium is realized upon the point of the maximum average return of credits, regardless of any excessive credit demands. As discussed in previous chapters, state-owned banks in China bear the responsibility of providing credit support to in-system outputs, so the supply of credits by state-owned banks is decided by the practical demand on credits during the gradual transition of the economy instead of the interest rate or the average return of credits. In other words, high economic

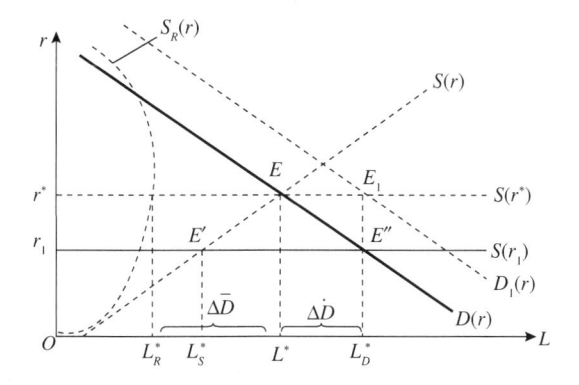

Figure 6.5 Credit equilibrium model of state-owned banks

growth constitutes the major factor that decides the credit supply by state-owned banks. It means that the credit equilibrium model of state-owned banks in China is different from the neoclassical model and the credit rationing model. As indicated in Figure 6.5, the curve of credit supply by state-owned banks is $S(r_I)$, which is parallel to the horizontal axis. This curve is below the equilibrium interest rate (i.e., the market interest rate r^*) due to financial restraint (see Chapter 5).

Next we discuss the government-intervention credit equilibrium model. As pointed out already, government intervention will lead to artificial shortage of credit supply. As the interest rate is depressed to a low level, the low interest rate stimulates the credit demand and inhibits the credit supply. The typical government-intervention credit equilibrium point is E', while the corresponding credit supply is L_S^* and the interest rate is the lower r_I. However, in China, based on the rigid demand on credits (the credit demand will be more flexible in the government-intervention credit equilibrium model) by the production sector (mainly state-owned enterprises), state-owned banks are obliged to provide financial support. Then, distinguished from the government-intervention model, the credit equilibrium of state-owned banks is decided by the intersect E'' of the curve $S(r_I)$ and the curve of credit demand $D(r)$. The practical credit supply is L_D^* upon the equilibrium. In other words, only the credit supply of L_D^* can assure the stable growth of in-system outputs.

Thus follows several interesting things. First, the credit supply observes the short edge rule (credit rule) in the typical government-intervention model, while it follows the long edge rule (debit rule) in the state-owned banks credit equilibrium model. Second, seen from Figure 6.5, upon the credit equilibrium point of state-owned banks, the credit supply is greater than that in the prior three credit equilibrium models, that is, $L_D^* > L^* > L_S^* > L_R^*$, which exactly matches practical conditions. Moreover, the state-owned banks credit equilibrium point shows the longest distance to the credit rationing equilibrium point, implying the difficulty of commercialization of state-owned banks. As pointed out in Chapter 3, national-ized state-owned banks are needed in the gradual reform rather than commer-cialized state-owned banks, as the former provide more credits than the latter. It is further proved by the discussion here. Third, as the credit demand is rigid in the credit equilibrium model of state-owned banks, the interest rate does not exert significant influence on credit demand. Even when the interest rate is raised to the higher r^*, the credit demand is still maintained at the high L_D^*, but the credit equilibrium point is moved upward from E'' to E_I.[4] On this basis, we can further extend the connotation of bad debts in Figure 6.1. When the credit equilibrium point is moved to E_I, by comparing the market interest rate r^* in Figure 6.5 to the market interest rate r_2 in Figure 6.1, it seems that state-owned banks bring back the credit surpluses originally given to state-owned enterprises due to the rise of the interest rate, which means that, theoretically, state-owned banks no longer have operating losses and bad debts. However, since the credit demand of state-owned enterprises is rigid, the rise of the interest rate only reflects the rise of credit return of state-owned banks, but this part of return has not been recorded in the account book and is actually virtual. More importantly, Figure 6.1 is prepared based on the neoclassical hypotheses, where the credit demand is sensitive and flexible to the interest rate, so when the interest rate rises from r_I to r_2, or when S^P moves upward to S^M, it signifies the disappearance of bad debts. However, in fact, in case of rigid credit demand (inflexible to the interest rate), bad debts still exist even if the inter-est rate is raised to the monopoly level (r_3 in Figure 6.1). No matter how high the interest rate is, state-owned enterprises exposed to soft budgetary restraints will still apply for loans because they never plan to repay these loans. State-owned enterprises in China bear responsibilities only for the profits but not the losses. After acquiring loans, some enterprises reject to make investments according to the proposal but apply them to projects of high risk and high return. If the project succeeds, they earn great profits, but if the project fails, the loss is borne by the state-owned bank. Then, the bad debts are produced (Yi Gang, 1996b). In Figure 6.5, if the interest rate is r^*, the possible scale of bad debts is $L_D^* - L_R^*$, or $\Delta \bar{D} + \Delta \dot{D}$, which equals ΔL^S in Figure 6.1 (b), that is, the credit supply in the credit equilib-rium model of state-owned banks minus the credit supply in the credit rationing equilibrium model. Therefore, these loans are exposed to great credit risk and will be less likely repaid.

III   Two forms of bad debts

In view of these discussions, as the credit equilibrium of state-owned banks fol-lows the long edge rule, the state has to supply successive credits to maintain the stable growth of in-system outputs and gradual transition in case of rigid credit demand. Especially after government appropriations were replaced by loans in 1985, the loans provided by state-owned banks to state-owned enterprises incor-porate a part of fiscal investment, mainly manifested by the policy-related loans from state-owned enterprises. State-owned banks have become the executor of the stable macroeconomic reform and policies on the industrial structure adjustment for the central government. Therefore, among the total credit supply L_D^* provided by state-owned banks, a considerable part is provided by state-owned banks as the financial agent of the government to cooperate with economic growth and stable transition. This is the part where bad debts are most likely produced. As the supply of this part of credit is decided by external factors, that is, the economic program of the state and its implementation method as well as the degree of materialization by governments at all levels (or magnification by local governments) (Xie Ping & Yu Qiao, 1996), the generation of bad debts cannot be explained by the credit behaviors of state-owned banks. Moreover, this type of credit is generally provided without any mortgage, so state-owned banks cannot unilaterally reduce or recover the loans or conduct reserve control unless the state adopts tight economic policies. This type of bad debts is tentatively referred to here as a kind of external bad debts or policy-related bad debts and is generally compulsory, intentional and predictable. These debts are originally attributed to rational efficiency loss allowed in the property right structure of state-owned banks (Zhang Jie, 1997b). From the perspective of the state, the efficiency loss is meanwhile the return in gradual transition and financial support. Table 6.3 presents the details of policy-related loans of

Table 6.3 Policy-related loans of state-owned banks: 1979–1996

	Total amount of policy-related loans (billion Yuan)	Total amount of loans of state-owned banks (billion Yuan)	Percentage of policy-related loans in total loans of state-owned banks (%)	Growth rate of policy-related loans (%)	Growth rate of loans of state-owned banks (%)	Total amount of loans provided by the central bank to state-owned banks (billion Yuan)	Percentage of loans from the central bank in policy-related loans (%)
1979	1.185	204.0	0.60	–	–		
1980	33.360	241.4	13.82	2715.19	18.33		
1981	43.226	276.5	15.63	29.57	14.54		
1982	52.537	305.2	17.21	21.54	10.38		
1983	56.922	343.1	16.59	8.35	12.42		
1984	126.621	442.0	28.65	122.45	28.83		
1985	185.770	590.6	31.45	46.71	33.62	219.318	118.06
1986	234.036	759.0	30.83	25.98	28.51	264.999	113.23
1987	277.683	903.2	30.74	18.65	19.00	241.960	87.14
1988	328.682	1,024.570	32.08	18.37	13.44	339.588	103.32
1989	425.121	1,206.4	35.24	29.34	17.75	432.550	101.75
1990	545.921	1,475.980	36.99	28.42	22.35	523.471	95.89
1991	678.170	1,759.480	38.54	24.22	19.21	607.510	86.93

(Continued)

Table 6.3 (Continued)

	Total amount of policy-related loans (billion Yuan)	Total amount of loans of state-owned banks (billion Yuan)	Percentage of policy-related loans in total loans of state-owned banks (%)	Growth rate of policy-related loans (%)	Growth rate of loans of state-owned banks (%)	Total amount of loans provided by the central bank to state-owned banks (billion Yuan)	Percentage of loans from the central bank in policy-related loans (%)
1992	741.090	2,108.170	35.15	9.28	19.82	698.0	78.03
1993	932.260	2,586.970	36.04	25.80	22.71	961.0	83.93
1994	1,148.520	3,244.120	35.40	23.20	25.40	1,045.0	71.30
1995	1,415.970	3,924.960	36.08	23.29	20.99	1,151.0	62.83
1996	1,644.010	4,743.470	34.66	16.10	20.85	1,451.840	63.40

Data source: Table 17.2 and 17.7 of Xiao Geng (1997), Table B of Appendix of this book, Table 15 of the World Bank (1996b), Table 3.3 of *China Financial Outlook* (1997) and *China Financial Yearbook* (1994–1997).

state-owned banks from 1979 to 1996.[5] Seen from the table, the policy-related loans of state-owned banks only amounted to 1.185 billion Yuan in 1979, accounting for 0.6% of total loans of state-owned banks, compared to 31.45% in 1985. By 1996, the policy-related loans amounted to as high as 1,644.010 billion Yuan, accounting for 34.66% of total loans of state-owned banks.

As policy-related loans occupy such a high proportion in total credits provided by state-owned banks and there is a high possibility of bad debts for policy-related loans, state-owned banks inevitably have a huge amount of policy-related bad debts. In accordance with the investigation and analysis in Xiao Geng (1997), default and overdue policy-related loans are very common, although they may not seem serious in the official account books of banks. Borrowers often use new loans to repay the old loans or apply the short-term circulating fund loan to the long-term investment projects, so state-owned banks do not regard the loan repayment ratio as a very useful index of loan performance ability (page 394–395). This means that we shall not consider the loan repayment ratio in the account books of state-owned banks as the direct criterion for judgment of bad debts. In this investigation and analysis report, Xiao Geng listed the accumulated loan repayment ratio of the Agricultural Bank of China and Rural Credit Cooperative between 1980 and 1990. The repayment ratio of total loans for fixed assets (including non-policy-related loans) of the Agricultural Bank of China was 55.5% in 1990, and the repayment ratio of total loans for current assets was 88.98%, including the repayment ratio of 82% for policy-related loans such as loans for procurement of agricultural products, 38% for subsidized poverty alleviation loans and 45.78% for FX RMB loans. By comparison, the loan repayment ratio of the Rural Credit Cooperative was higher than the ratio of same type of loans of the Agricultural Bank of China. It implies that the performance of policy-related loans is worse than other loans. The bad debts among policy-related loans of state-owned banks cannot be listed here due to a lack of relevant information, but some assumptions and speculations still make sense here. If one assumes that the average repayment ratio of policy-related loans of state-owned banks was 70%,[6] then the bad debts among policy-related loans of state-owned banks reached 493.203 billion Yuan in 1996.

It shall be noted that state-owned banks generally have no control over the release of most policy-related loans. As the purpose and even the borrowing enterprises of loans have been designated by the state or central bank prior, the state-owned banks will follow the decision no matter if they wish to do so. As pointed out in Chapter 2, a considerable part of funds among the policy-related loans released by state-owned banks are issued in a form of re-loans from the central bank (the fund sources for re-loans are mainly the reserves submitted by state-owned banks). As analyzed in Xie Ping (1996), most credits of the central bank were applied to policy-related loans before 1993. For instance, the proportion of new re-loans provided by the central bank to state-owned banks applied to policy-related projects was 83.2% in 1989, compared to 93.8% in 1990 and 100% in 1991 (pages 11–12). As shown in Table 6.3, the amount of policy-related loans of state-owned banks approaches the amount of loans rendered by the central bank to state-owned banks from 1985 to 1993, which is not a coincidence, as analyzed prior. After 1994, the credits of the central bank occupied a decreasing proportion in policy-related loans, mainly due to the rise of proportion of foreign exchanges. According to statistics, the proportion of foreign exchanges in net increase of assets of the central bank grew from 7% in 1993 to 75% in 1994, while the proportion of the credits rendered by the central bank to the banking system (mainly state-owned banks) in net increase of assets declined from 78% in 1993 to 20% in 1994 (Xie Ping & Yu Qiao, 1996). This also means that the decline of loans of the central bank does not necessarily represent the decline of demand on policy-related loans of the state. Therefore, if the legal reserve ratio is not correspondingly lowered,[7] state-owned banks need to invest extra funds on policy-related credits. It further proves that the policy-related bad debts in the account books of state-owned banks show no direct connection to the credit behaviors of state-owned banks. In a strict sense, they do not belong to the real bad debts of banks.

If the state exerts complete control over behaviors of state-owned banks and applies all credits to the purposes designated by the state, all possible bad debts of state-owned banks will become policy-related bad debts under these circumstances. However, the question arises in that state control over credits of state-owned banks is not complete and is even relaxing along with the reform. Credits behaviors of state-owned bank are increasingly exposed to the influence of local preferences and preferences of state-owned banks. Therefore, other forms of bad debts of state-owned banks may arise, such as the commercial form. Based on the dilemma of property rights of state-owned banks discussed earlier, the possibility of commercial debts will gradually rise along with the reform. As super state-owned enterprises protected by the government, state-owned banks are subject to severe soft budgetary restraint and probably will take the credit risk to pursue maximum short-term benefits. In other words, relying on the advantage in public financial property rights, state-owned banks may have risks externalized. As their credit behaviors are free from the internal restraint of credit rationing (in a standard sense), they may be easily attracted by the high interest rate and profit opportunities and thus lead to a great amount of commercial bad debts. The key to the issue does not lie in whether state-owned banks follow the regulations of the central bank on loan but in the fundamental contradiction between the property right structure of state-owned banks and their expanding control over credits. The former issue can be settled by establishing specialized policy banks, while the latter requires transformation of the financial property right structure. Risks and benefits must be internalized in the state based on the public financial property right structure of state-owned banks, but the emergence of private interests and expansion of the credit control of state-owned banks bring about externalization, that is, externalization of risks and internalization of benefits. The property right structure that has risks and benefits separated constitutes the fundamental cause for commercial bad debts of state-owned banks. Without changing the public financial property right structure, the more independent the credit behaviors of state-owned banks, the more likely that moral hazards will take place. Then state-owned banks will show increasing interest in credits of high profits, leading to the greater possibility of the generation of commercial bad debts. I once reached a conclusion in a research study (Zhang Jie, 1997b) that commercial bad debts of state-owned banks were the unnecessary cost for the state to carry out so-called marketization reform. More interestingly, policy-related bad debts are used as a cover for commercial debts by state-owned banks. They are finding ways and means to recognize the losses of commercial bad debts as policy-related bad debts. For example, in case of low profit of the state-owned bank, the bank may pass the buck to too many policy-related loans designated by the government or to default of state-owned enterprises. External variables such as government intervention, reform of state-owned enterprises, inflation-proof savings policies, natural and man-made calamities and even loan limitation may be blamed for the low efficiency of state-owned banks (Wu Xiaoling et al., 1997). More possibly, state-owned banks invest policy-related loans designated by the state to other sectors and press the central bank to constantly increase credits, thus leading to the simultaneous rise of policy-related and commercial bad debts.[8]

Also due to the property right structure, when the boundary of organizations of state-owned banks expands and the principal-agent chain extends too long, it is common that the agent twists behaviors or deviates from the principal's preference in credits. The inferior level of state-owned banks often makes use of the right to decide the limited credit funds to pursue private interests. In many cases, if rendering high kickbacks to the person holding the control right over credit funds at a certain level, the credit demand will be satisfied. According to the credit rationing equilibrium model, the credit-demanding party that pays high kickbacks often shows high risk preference or prepares to bet all on a single throw. The higher the kickbacks given to credit suppliers, the less possible the credit-demanding party will repay the debts, leading to a high possibility for the generation of commercial bad debts of state-owned banks. As a result, the single decision maker of bank credits suffers no loss (the loss goes to the whole state-owned bank), but the state bears rapidly increasing risk responsibility without limitation for state-owned banks. The shortage of in-system credits incurred by opportunistic behaviors of state-owned banks at the inferior level will finally be covered by the central bank constantly injecting new loans because in-system credit demand is rigid. As is known to us, whether the rigid credit demand can be satisfied is directly related to the success of the gradual reform.[9]

This discussion can be described with a simple model. In view of these discussions, the total scale of credits of state-owned banks L consist of two parts, the policy-related loan L^P and the spontaneous (or commercial) loan L^M. Since L is a given amount within a certain period, L^P and L^M are inversely proportional to each other:

$$L = \alpha L^M + (1 - \alpha)L^P \qquad (0 \leq \alpha \leq 1) \qquad (6.1)$$

The value of α is decided by the independent credit capability of state-owned banks. The policy-related loans are provided at a price of r^P, while the price for the spontaneous loan tends to be r^M. r^M is higher than r^P. Ignoring the financing cost, then:

$$\pi L^M \cdot L^P = \alpha L^M \cdot r^M + (1 - \alpha) L^P \cdot r^P \qquad (6.2)$$

π is the benefit of state-owned banks. Obtain L^P and L^M from equation (6.1) and respectively substitute the values into equation (6.2),

$$\begin{cases} \pi L^P = L \cdot r^M + (1-\alpha)L^P(r^P - r^M) \\ \pi L^M = L \cdot r^P = \alpha L^M (r^M - r^P) \end{cases} \qquad (6.3)$$

The following first-order condition shall be satisfied for state-owned banks to realize maximum benefits:

$$\pi L^{M'} = \alpha(r^M - r^P) = 0$$

i.e.

$$r^M = r^P \qquad (6.4)$$

Then substitute equation (6.4) into equation (6.3),

$$\text{Max}\pi_M^L = L \cdot r^M \qquad (6.5)$$

It suggests that, for state-owned banks, all credits shall be provided at the market interest rate to attain the maximum benefit. The equation for the maximum benefit of state-owned banks can be acquired the same way:

$$\text{Max}\pi L^P = L \cdot r^P \tag{6.6}$$

It means that, for the state, state-owned banks shall provide all credits completely following the interest rate and purpose designated by the central bank (or central government) to realize the maximum benefits during the gradual transition. This idea can be illustrated with Figure 6.6 (a).

If we suppose the normal credit supply of state-owned banks as L^* (the normal credit supply here refers to the part of credits that render financial support to the gradual transition and can be repaid), both the commercial loan and policy-related loan shall be no larger than L_D^* in scale. The following conclusions can be drawn from Figure 6.6. (1) If all credits of state-owned banks are policy-related loans ($\alpha = 0$), the abnormal credits of ΔL^P may appear theoretically. These abnormal credits may possibly become policy-related bad debts. (2) If all credits are allocated by state-owned banks pursuant to their own willingness ($\alpha = 1$) upon the current property right structure of state-owned banks, the abnormal credits of ΔL^M may appear theoretically, leading to a great quantity of commercial bad debts. (3) Since state-owned banks provide both commercial and policy-related loans, bad debts must be a combination of commercial and policy-related bad debts. Therefore, the function of credit provision of state-owned bank shows discontinuity within the certain interval of $L^* L_D^*$, as indicated in Figure 6.6 (b). In Figure 6.6 (b), the

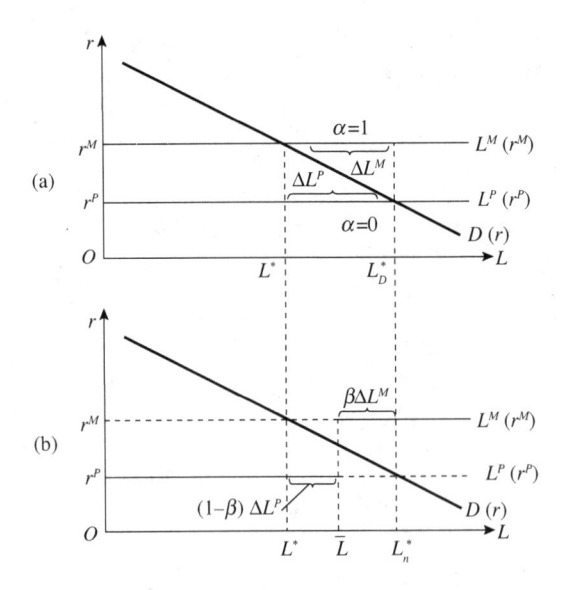

Figure 6.6 Dual model of bad debts

combined point of the two types of loans is located at point $\bar{L}$. Supposing the provisions of two credits between the interval of $L^* L_D^*$ are inversely proportional to each other,[10] the credit provision by state-owned banks at point $\bar{L}$ can be represented with:

$$L_D^* = L^* + \beta \triangle L^M + (1-\beta)\triangle L^P \qquad (0 \le \beta \le 1) \qquad (6.7)$$

As with α, the value of β is decided by the independent credit ability of state-owned banks, which further determines the specific location of $\bar{L}$ in the interval $L^* L_D^*$.

3   About the solution of capital injection

I   Dual capital injection of debts

As pointed out previously, the capital structure of state-owned banks features a unique phenomenon, the virtual capital. This is the key factor that determines the path for the institutional changes of state-owned banks in China. To be specific, the virtual capital refers to the concept that the state, the contributor and owner, applies the comparative advantage of the violence potential as the capital share instead of directly injecting the real capital. State-owned banks rely on the special capital share to replace or arrange for the real capital structure. I regarded it as the "guarantee replacing capital injection" in a special research (Zhang Jie 1997b). State-owned banks are largely relying on the capital injection of guarantee to sustain the credit supply against the rapid decline of the capital ratio. For example, the net asset ratio of state-owned banks dropped from 6.41% in 1990 to 5.48% in 1996. Meanwhile, the average growth rate of credit supply had maintained as high as 21.62% from 1990 to 1996, including the average growth rate of policy-related loans reaching 21.47% (see Table 6.3). This reveals the significance of the capital injection of guarantee to supporting the capital structure of state-owned banks in China and the gradual transition. Along with the further development of reform, the capital injection of guarantee will become increasingly important.

Even though guarantee can replace capital injection, it shall be manifested by real capital in real economic life. A real capital carrier is demanded as state-owned banks cannot directly lend the state guarantee to state-owned enterprises, although the injection of real capital (i.e., provision of credits) is a kind of guarantee itself. What can play the role as the carrier of real capital for the capital injection of guarantee during the reform? The answer is obvious: the household deposits (i.e., financial surpluses). As a result of a series of special financial arrangements, household deposits are gathered by state-owned banks. These special financial arrangements have practically laid an institutional foundation for the capital injection of substitution. The reason is clear. Only when most household deposits are collected by state-owned banks through the monopolistic state-owned financial institutional arrangements under state control can the capital injection of guarantee by the state be realized. Therefore, after government appropriations were replaced by loans in 1985, it seemed that the state attempted to impose costs on state-owned enterprises for the use of state-owned capital thus to improve the efficiency of capital use, but the state was actually changing the way of capital injection to relieve the fiscal pressure of the state.

As pointed out in previous discussions, China has featured a weak treasury and strong finance during the gradual reform of China. The decline of state capacity resulting from the decline of the fiscal capacity of the state has been rapidly made up by effective financial control by the state. Financial control by the state has covered the weak capital injection incurred by decline of the fiscal capacity of the state. Although the state is incapable of directly injecting capital to state-owned enterprises (including state-owned banks), it is capable of providing guarantee. Based on the state guarantee, state-owned banks already embrace a part of capital injected by the state by absorbing deposits. Therefore, all state-owned banks are trying their best to compete for household savings, as more deposits absorbed indicate more capital injection of guarantee from the state. For state-owned banks, the direct capital injection from the state treasury and the attraction of deposits under state guarantee present the same utility (Zhang Jie, 1997b). Theoretically, the shares where deposits replace the capital injection within the capital structure of state-owned banks approximately equal the value of state-owned capital that should be injected to state-owned banks by the state calculated based on the net worth, or, in other words, equal to the scale of virtual capital that the state should replace by injecting real capital. According to Table 6.1, the scale reached 639.420 billion Yuan in 1996, accounting for 12.89% of total deposits of state-owned banks of the year and approximately 18% of urban and rural household deposits. Theoretically, since the state-owned banks have little self-owned capital, about 18% of household deposits will immediately transfer to be the bad debts of savers (creditors) after they enter the state-owned banks. These bad debts do not go wrong (i.e., a run on banks is not triggered among savers) apparently because of the guarantee by the state (i.e., the cashing commitment). This is another unique characteristic of the financial institutional structure during the gradual reform of China that state-owned banks borrow from savers for capital injection of debts during the gradual reform.

Based on the special connotation and formation mechanism of the capital structure of state-owned banks, only the state, the owner and controller, can represent the property rights of state-owned banks. This is simply because, as the representative of property rights of state-owned banks, it should be capable of buying the part of capital injection to state-owned banks (i.e., replacing it with the real capital) that the state replaces with guarantee based on its natural advantage (combining with household deposits). As no one possesses the guarantee capability as the state does, so it has to acquire financial property rights by transacting with the real capital. Then again, even the state itself cannot supply enough funds to purchase its guarantee. In this case, a material issue for the reform of state-owned banks lies in how to restore the virtual capital under state guarantee to be the real capital. Therefore, we always believe that the special capital structure of state-owned banks decides the reform method of state-owned banks. The key to the reform of state-owned banks shall be what it can do upon its capital structure and property rights structure instead of what we want it to do (Zhang Jie, 1997b). In other words, the path of reform of state-owned banks directly depends on the process of replacing the virtual capital with the real capital as well as the conflicts of interest, bargaining and benefit-cost ratio of different interested parties during the process.

Furthermore, the most attractive part in the overall institutional arrangements made by the state during the previous gradual transition shall be the capital structure centering on capital injection of debts of state-owned banks. It is subtle that when this special capital structure is established, capital injection from savers (a kind of non-state-owned sector) does not change the property right structure of state-owned banks. This is because however large proportion the capital injection of debts occupies in the capital structure, it is merely a kind of creditor's right but not ownership. In this way, on one hand, the state does not need to directly pay for the cost and thus avoids fiscal pressure; on the other hand, the state does not give up the state-owned financial property rights or financial control. Savers do not acquire the state-owned financial property rights even though they take out the money. More interestingly, despite the huge scale of total deposits from all savers, savers are widely dispersed. Each of them possesses only a very small part of creditor's right, so it is difficult to organize the collective activities among savers to change the property right structure of state-owned banks or to force state-owned banks to change their behaviors or financial property rights structure by withdrawing deposits. Does it mean that if savers cooperate with each other and organize collective activities, a real no-state-owned force of capital will be formed, thus to change or threaten the property right structure of state-owned banks? Or will it become another feasible approach of the reform of the property right structure of state-owned banks? This question will be discussed later. Anyhow, the special structure of state-owned financial property rights (or capital structure) in China that separates the property right owner and the real contributor has achieved great success in the previous process of gradual reform.

It is also noteworthy that state-owned enterprises are also exposed to a situation similar to the capital structure of state-owned banks. As mentioned, the capital injection to state-owned enterprises by the state has been also rapidly declining since the reform. As shown in Table 4.1, the investment by the state treasury on production of state-owned enterprises accounted for 92.3% in 1972, which was lowered to 32.5% in 1986 and 15.4% in 1996. The decline of the fiscal investment has been covered by state-owned banks. Therefore, the capital structure of state-owned enterprises also incorporates the capital injection of debts, that is, the credit funds from state-owned banks replacing the capital injection by the state treasury to state-owned enterprises. The loan for fixed assets provided by state-owned banks amounted to only 0.79 billion Yuan in 1979, the beginning of the reform, but had grown to 100.59 billion Yuan by 1986 and later to 1,203.420 billion Yuan by 1996, when the financing for fixed capital provided by state-owned banks to state-owned enterprises took up approximately 60%. Moreover, the accumulated loans for current capital only reached 203.17 billion Yuan in 1979, compared to 658.49 billion Yuan in 1986 and 3,540.05 billion Yuan in 1996. After 1985, the credits provided by state-owned banks have occupied about 94% of all current

Table 6.4 Changes of the asset-liability ratio of state-owned industrial enterprises of China

(%)							
1980	*1990*	*1991*	*1992*	*1993*	*1994*	*1995*	*1996*
18.7	58.4	60.5	61.5	71.7	75.1	74.2	78.0

Data source and note: Data of 1995 are introduced from Lu Liling and Shen Ying (1997, page 24), and data of 1996 are calculated based on relevant information in the *China Statistical Yearbook* (1997). The theoretical realm holds very different opinions on calculation of the asset-liability ratio of state-owned industrial enterprises. With the data of 1993 as an example, some people took the identified asset losses and hidden losses into consideration and attained the practical asset-liability ratio of 83.3% (Zhang Chunlin, 1996). The table here only lists one of those different estimates.

capital on average, resulting in the high-debt structure of state-owned enterprises that people often talk about. See details in Table 6.4.

Apparently, the key to the issue lies in the capital structure (property right structure) of the enterprise behind the high asset-liability ratio instead of how high the ratio is. The high asset-liability ratio does not necessarily lead to debt struggles of state-owned enterprises. It only becomes a problem when the capital structure of state-owned enterprises is exposed to certain issues. In terms of the capital structure of state-owned enterprises, the state has held its preference for single state-owned capital during the gradual reform. Undoubtedly, the state-owned property right structure is appropriate for many state-owned enterprises in view of their operating characteristics (such as infrastructure or public business). Generally, the state has strictly controlled the access of non-state-owned sectors to the capital structure of state-owned enterprises as the owner during the reform because, once control is relaxed, they will impact the public property right structure of state-owned enterprises and be unfavorable for state control over property right forms and acquisition of benefits (over 80% of fiscal revenues of the state rely on these state-owned enterprises). The state does not have enough funds to invest and is meanwhile unwilling to open the capital market of state-owned enterprises (i.e., the property right market) and therefore has the only way out, that is, financing through borrowing. In the existing financial institutional framework, only state-owned banks can provide financing to state-owned enterprises. Providing debt financing to state-owned enterprises through the state-owned financial channel makes no difference with state-owned banks making use of state guarantee to realize capital injection of deposits (debts). Without changing the property right (capital) structure of state-owned enterprises, the state enables a great quantity of capital injection and financial support to state-owned enterprises and thus realizes dual goals during the gradual reform, the growth of in-system outputs and state control over the return from outputs.

Under these circumstances, the credit supply by state-owned banks to state-owned enterprises somewhat indicates the capital injection by the state to state-owned enterprises (replacing fiscal investment). The state provides enough guarantees to state-owned banks and establishes a strong finance so that these banks can cope with the capital difficulties of state-owned enterprises. Here it can be easily seen that the subtle pattern of dual capital injection of debts during the gradual reform of China is an extremely original and excellent institutional arrangement. Since the reform was initiated, a great amount of gains from monetization were produced. Since these gains, particularly financial surpluses, were distributed in a very decentralized manner, the key difficulty lies in how to finally inject these surpluses to the state-owned economy and form financial support without changing the property right structure of the state-owned economy. Then, the state-owned financial institutional arrangement reveals its unique function. First, it made use of its comparative advantage by expanding the scale of organizations to expand the scale of savings, rapidly collected several trillion Yuan in banks and then had the state provide the full-amount guarantee. When this institutional arrangement was established, the state-owned economy was able to acquire reliable fund support essential for economic growth without changing the state-owned property rights. No matter how much it cost to realize the institutional arrangement during the reform, it was undoubtedly rational only if it complied with the logic of gradual reform. We shall not judge an institutional arrangement or reform path without considering the logic of the gradual reform.

Since state-owned banks practically inject capital to state-owned enterprises by providing credits, it is logical for state-owned enterprise to consider a part of the credits of state-owned banks as self-owned capital. In other words, after the credits are transferred to state-owned enterprises, fund users never planned to make repayment at all. Or, as the credit funds injected to state-owned enterprises are fundamentally the state-owned capital, they are doomed to become the bad debts of state-owned banks (Zhang Jie, 1997b). For state-owned banks, these credit funds have already lost their liquidity. Therefore, most bad debts of state-owned banks (mainly the policy-related bad debts) shall not be considered as bad debts in a strict sense.

II Whether capital injection can improve the capital structure of state-owned banks

As discussed prior, if the state can restore the capital structure of state-owned banks, state-owned banks will continue to reflect the utility function and preference of the state, when the policy-related credits will still be provided and policy-related bad debts will still exist. At the same time, the state still bears the final risk responsibility and continues to control state-owned banks due to no change of the capital structure. And this leads to the problem. As state-owned banks are still exposed to externalization, and the restored boundary of state-owned financial property rights are huge, the state is incapable of preventing and controlling the opportunistic behaviors of state-owned banks (as well as local factors). It means that the probability of occurrence of commercial bad debts continues as always. Even if the state can eliminate the static bad debts at a certain time, the restored capital structure cannot remove the foundation of property rights giving rise to the generation of bad debts. Under these circumstances, the capital structure will still be damaged after a certain period, so the state, as the contributor and final risk undertaker, has to invest on restoration again, until the state has no money to invest. Therefore, the fundamental issue is not about whether the state can afford it or not but about how to fundamentally solve the issue of the capital structure of state-owned banks and to seek a new contributor and risk undertaker.[11]

If the state is capable of injecting capital to state-owned banks (or state-owned enterprises) to restore their capital structure, it means that the state is also capable of providing guarantee. The key is that the capital injection by the state is a kind of free capital or risk-free capital for state-owned banks, no matter whether it is capital injection in the form of deposits under state guarantee (virtual capital) of the injection of real capital. The state only changes the form of the free capital by replacing the original virtual capital with direct investment. As a matter of fact, it is the same with capital injection by the state on state-owned enterprises or reduction of the asset-liability ratio of state-owned enterprises, as the capital injection only increases the proportion of free capital but fails to touch or solve the fundamental problem (Zhang Chunlin, 1996). Although the capital ratio (or asset-liability ratio) increases (or declines) due to capital injection to state-owned banks (or state-owned enterprises), suggesting the improvement of the capital structure of state-owned banks, it is still the state that bears the risks and finally settles the losses (but not the state-owned banks). Therefore, for state-owned banks, the use of the capital injected finds no difference with the virtual capital before replacement. Since the state is still the contributor, state-owned banks still tend to apply the new capital injected to expanding the credit supply, thus lowering the asset ratio and then requiring capital injection again. Obviously, capital injection by the state cannot restore the capital structure and leads to constant expansion of credit provision and bad debts, particularly commercial bad debts. It does not make sense to unilaterally pursue the capital adequacy ratio when the state acts as the final risk undertaker. The significance of the capital adequacy ratio will only be revealed when the state is no longer the final risk undertaker. The main goal of the capital adequacy ratio is to prevent potential financial risk, that is, the crisis of the run on banks. But in China, the state bears the final obligation in cashing. In the state-owned financial capital structure, the cashing capability of the state and people's confidence in the state matter the most instead of the capital adequacy ratio of state-owned banks. The real problem with state-owned banks lies in too centralized financial risks rather than the simple insufficient capital adequacy ratio. The insufficient capital adequacy ratio can be temporarily solved by state financing, but the centralized risks and low efficiency cannot be relieved through capital injection by the state.

Furthermore, based on capital injection by the state, the financial property rights of state-owned banks still go to the public (or state), so the state, as the owner, still has state-owned banks follow the state preference in businesses and sets up the incentives and restraints for state-owned banks that reflect the utility function of the state. Therefore, the state has to realize the economic and social goals of the state at a cost of low allocation efficiency and X efficiency, such as rapid economic growth, full employment, inflation inhibition, safeguarding social stability and so on. No matter how much the state wants to have state-owned banks observe the utility function of the state in businesses, the property right structure has decided the rules on behaviors of state-owned banks. Under the public financial property rights, the state cannot protect the state-owned financial property rights by exercising the exit right as the investor and contributor. In other words, when discovering the low allocation efficiency and X efficiency of state-owned banks, the state cannot threat them with exit (such as clearing up bad debts or advocating bankruptcy) because state-owned banks are aware that the potential cost will be higher if the state exercises the exit right. The state also cannot threaten them with transfer of financial property rights, as the state's right to acquire surpluses is nontransferable and inseparable. Then, the rational reaction of state-owned banks is to make use of the weakness of the state where the state cannot impose punishment by exiting as well as the information asymmetry to conduct opportunistic behaviors that acquire maximum private interests but may damage the state-owned property rights, leaving a great quantity of commercial bad debts to the state. Therefore, it is only wishful thinking to help state-owned banks establish a complete state-owned capital structure through capital injection and have these banks operate based on commercialization rules. Commercialized operation of state-owned banks can only be realized upon separable and tradable financial property rights.

Notes

1 See discussions on segmentation of ownerships and property rights in Zhang Jie (1994).
2 Dai Xianglong, the former president of the People's Bank of China, pointed out at a press conference at the beginning of 1998 that the loans that could not be recovered (i.e., bad debts) in China only occupied 5% to 6% of total loans, with 30 billion Yuan already written off in 1997 and with 50 billion Yuan to be written off in 1998 and 60 billion Yuan to be written off in 1999 and 2000. He believed that the capital adequacy ratio of state-owned banks could attain 8% at least by 1999.
3 See details in Zhang Weiying (1996, pages 562–569)
4 According to an investigation against factory directors and managers of 300 state-owned large and medium-sized enterprises, 83.3% of directors and managers would not reduce the loan when the interest rate was increased by 5%, and 64.3% of directors and managers would not reduce the loan when the interest rate was increased by 10% (Fan Gang et al., 1990, page 257).
5 See more details of policy-related loans of state-owned banks in Xiao Geng (1997, Page 361–418)
6 The average repayment ratio of 70% may be overestimated considering the extremely low repayment ratio for the loans to support key state-owned enterprises, to clear debt chain and to support unprofitable enterprises released by state-owned banks. These loans are actually applied as relief, the same with the poverty alleviation loan of the Agricultural Bank of China, so the repayment ratio should be the same.
7 The legal deposit reserve ratio was lowered from the previous 13% to 8% by the central bank on March 25, 1998.
8 For an instance, the banking system invested a large quantity of funds on the real estate and stocks markets through interbank lending between 1992 and 1993, leading to a serious lack of funds for key construction projects of the state and procurement of

agricultural and sideline products. The central bank had to increase policy-related loans (Xie Ping & Yu Qiao, 1996).

9 It shall be noted that the out-plan credit impulse of state-owned banks enables a part of financial resources to flow to non-state-owned enterprises and support their outputs growth, which can be considered another kind of contribution to the gradual transition. Meanwhile, the low-interest-rate policy of state-owned banks has encouraged the non-priority sector (non-state-owned sector) to make irrational capital investment and rapidly lowered their capital efficiency (Xiao Geng, 1997, pages 402–417).

10 In fact, as discussed prior, ΔL^M and ΔL^P are not simply inversely proportional to each other, but the former may promote the latter to expand together. This effect is ignored here for the convenience of analysis, but it has no effect on the conclusion of the analysis.

11 Wu Xiaoling et al. (1995) and Zhou Xiaochuan et al. (1994) once held that the state should solve it through direct capital injection but apparently ignored the significance of the changes of the financial property right structure.

Appendix

Benefit and cost of financial control by the state: item data

Table A SE: 1979–1996

	M (billion Yuan)	P (%)	SE (billion Yuan)
1979	26.77	102	5.641
1980	34.62	106	7.406
1981	39.62	102.4	4.883
1982	43.91	101.9	4.210
1983	52.98	101.5	8.936
1984	79.21	102.8	25.516
1985	195	108.8	106.425
1986	242	106.0	44.340
1987	272	107.3	27.959
1988	358	118.5	72.574
1989	442	117.8	71.307
1990	577	102.1	132.223
1991	717	102.9	136.054
1992	854	105.4	129.981
1993	1,134	113.2	247.350
1994	1,474	121.7	279.376
1995	1,721	114.8	215.157
1996	2,379	106.1	620.170

Data source and note: (1) M is monetary base, including M_0 between 1979 and 1984. The data of M_0 and P (price index) between 1979 and 1990 are introduced from Table 8.1 and 8.2 of Yi Gang (1996a). (2) The data of M between 1985 and 1995 refer to Table 15 of the World Bank (1996b). (3) The data of M in 1996 and P from 1991 to 1996 are quoted from Table 3.1 and 3.3 of *China Financial Outlook* (1997). (4) The M_0 in 1978 is 21.2 billion Yuan. (5) M = money in circulation + legal reserves + deposits at financial organizations.

Table B BT: 1979–1996

	L (billion Yuan)	L_r (%)	L_i (billion Yuan)	S (billion Yuan)	S_r (%)	S_i (billion Yuan)	MC_r (%)	BC0 (billion Yuan)	MC (billion Yuan)	BP (billion Yuan)	BT (billion Yuan)
	(1)	(2)	(3)	(4)	(5)	(6)	(7)	(8)	(9)	(10)	(11)
			(1) × (2)			(4) × (5)			(7) × (8)	(3) − (6) − (9)	
1979	204.0	4.32	8.813	134.0	3.96	5.306	0.2	216.3	0.432	3.075	0.615
1980	241.4	4.32	10.428	165.9	5.40	8.959	0.2	262.4	0.525	0.944	0.189
1981	276.5	4.32	11.945	200.6	5.40	10.832	0.25	304.8	0.762	0.351	0.217
1982	305.2	5.76	17.58	228.7	5.76	13.173	0.3	341.5	1.025	3.382	2.367
1983	343.1	5.76	19.763	267.6	5.76	15.414	0.3	388.5	1.166	3.183	2.562
1984	442.0	7.92	35.006	338.6	5.76	19.503	0.35	508.0	1.778	13.725	11.529
1985	590.6	10.8	63.785	427.3	6.84	29.227	0.5	643.1	3.216	31.342	25.074
1986	759.0	10.8	81.972	538.2	7.20	38.750	0.68	820.6	5.580	37.642	30.114
1987	903.2	10.8	97.546	657.2	7.20	47.318	0.76	997.6	7.582	42.646	34.117
1988	1,024.57	10.8	110.654	668.61	8.64	57.768	0.94	1,154.1	10.849	42.037	33.630
1989	1,206.4	10.8	130.291	798.23	11.34	90.519	0.89	1,361.8	12.120	27.652	19.356
1990	1,475.98	10.8	159.406	1,045.94	8.64	90.369	0.79	1,683.8	13.302	55.735	39.015
1991	1,759.48	9.0	158.353	1,329.97	7.56	100.546	0.80	2,061.4	16.491	41.316	28.921
1992	2,108.18	9.0	189.735	1,748.43	7.56	132.181	0.91	2,426.9	22.085	35.469	24.828
1993	2,586.97	12.24	316.645	2,140.01	10.98	234.973	1.00	2,987.2	29.872	51.800	36.260
1994	3,244.12	12.24	397.08	2,933.10	10.98	322.054	1.36	4,090.3	55.628	19.398	13.579
1995	3,924.96	13.5	529.87	3,878.26	10.98	425.833	1.36	5,138.2	59.880	44.157	30.910
1996	4,743.47	11.7	554.986	4,959.33	8.33	412.864	1.40	6,324.7	88.546	53.576	37.503

Data source and note: (1) This table is prepared based on relevant data in *China Financial Outlook* (1994–1997), Table 7 of *1978–1994 China Reform and Development Report: The Path of China*, Table 4.1 of Xie Ping (1996) and Table 6.7 of Wu Jiesi (1996). (2) In this table, L indicates the amount of loans of state-owned banks, L_r represents the interest rate for 3-year loan for fixed assets, L_i for the loan interest income, S for the amount of savings, S_r for the interest rate of 1-year fixed deposit, S_i for expenditure on deposit interest, MC_r for the ratio of operating cost of the bank to total assets, BC for bank assets, MC for the operating cost, BP for theoretical profit of state-owned banks and BT for estimate of fiscal contribution of state-owned banks. (3) The data of MC_r from 1979 to 1985 and in 1993, 1995 and 1996 are estimated by the author, while the ratios in other years are the average value of the four major state-owned banks. (4) BP is called the theoretical profit for two reasons, First, the calculation of the cost and benefit of banks in this table is rough. Second, the profits revealed in this table since the1990s are only the paper profits, but actually the interests of loans of many state-owned enterprises can hardly be recovered. For instance, the receivable but unreceived interest in 1996 reached as high as 118.5 billion Yuan. Considering this factor, the practical loss of banks this year attained 64.96 billion Yuan. (5) The S_r of 1996 is the average value between the interest rate of 9.18% on May 1 and 7.47% on Aug. 23. (6) Please be prudent when referring to data in this table. It would be better to verify the data against other materials.

Table C FS: 1979–1996

	FS/GDP (%)	GDP (billion Yuan)	FS (billion Yuan)
1979	5.5	216.3	11.897
1980	9.5	262.4	24.928
1981	6.9	304.8	21.031
1982	6.4	341.5	21.851
1983	5.6	388.5	21.756
1984	5.2	508.0	26.416
1985	4.8	643.1	30.869
1986	5.9	820.6	48.415
1987	8.4	1,130.7	94.979
1988	8.1	1,407.42	114.001
1989	8.9	1,599.76	142.379
1990	10.3	1,768.13	182.117
1991	8.7	2,161.78	188.075
1992	8.2	2,663.81	218.432
1993	9.8	3,463.44	339.417
1994	5.7	4,662.23	265.770
1995	5.7	5,826.05	332.085
1996	6.0	6,779.5	406.770

Data source and note: (1) The data of this table are calculated based on *China Statistical Yearbook* (1992); *China Financial Yearbook* (1992); the World Bank (1996b); *China Financial Outlook* (1994–1997) and *1978–1994 China Reform and Development Report: The Path of China* etc. (2) The FS/GDP between 1979 and 1986 only refers to the proportion of the treasury in assets of state-owned banks, while the data of GDP only refer to assets of state-owned banks of the current year. The calculation obviously underestimates the fiscal contribution of the finance. (3) The FS/GDP data in 1996 are estimated by the author.

Table D MC: 1979–1996

	MC_r (%)	BC (billion Yuan)	MC (billion Yuan)
1979	0.20	216.3	0.432
1980	0.20	262.4	0.525
1981	0.25	304.8	0.762
1982	0.30	341.5	1.025
1983	0.30	388.5	1.166
1984	0.35	508.0	1.778
1985	0.50	414.1	2.071
1986	0.68	537.6	3.656
1987	0.76	675.6	5.135

(*Continued*)

Table D (Continued)

	MC_r (%)	BC (billion Yuan)	MC (billion Yuan)
1988	0.94	748.1	7.032
1989	0.89	859.8	7.652
1990	0.79	1,026.8	8.112
1991	0.80	1,236.4	9.891
1992	0.91	1,455.9	13.249
1993	1.00	1,674.2	16.742
1994	1.36	2,368.3	32.209
1995	1.36	3,062.2	41.646
1996	1.40	3,635.8	50.901

Data source and note: (1) The data of this table is introduced from the corresponding items in Table B. (2) The values of *BC* between 1985 and 1996 have deducted the assets of the central bank from the values of BC in Table B, so the values of MC of corresponding years also decrease.

Table E SC: 1985–1996

	SC_r (%)	CBC (billion Yuan)	SC (billion Yuan)
1985	0.50	229.0	1.145
1986	0.68	283.0	1.924
1987	0.76	322.0	2.447
1988	0.94	406.0	3.816
1989	0.89	502.0	4.468
1990	0.79	657.0	5.190
1991	0.80	825.0	6.600
1992	0.91	971.0	8.836
1993	1.00	1,313.0	13.130
1994	1.36	1,722.0	23.419
1995	1.36	2,076.0	28.234
1996	1.40	2,688.85	37.644

Data source and note: (2) This table is calculated based on Table B here, Table 15 of the World Bank (1996b) and Table 3.3 and 3.7 of *China Financial Outlook* (1997). (2) SC_r in the table is the asset-cost ratio of the central bank and CBC is the assets of the central bank. (3) The *SC* values between 1979 and 1984 have been incorporated in the *MC* values in Table D. (4) This table represents the asset-cost ratio of the central bank with the asset-cost ratio of state-owned banks and uses the operating cost to represent the supervision cost. Direct reference to the data is not recommended.

Table F SI: 1979–1996

	S (billion Yuan)	S_r (%)	S_i (billion Yuan)
1979	28.10	3.96	1.113
1980	39.95	5.40	2.157
1981	52.37	5.40	2.828
1982	67.54	5.76	3.890
1983	89.25	5.76	5.141
1984	121.47	5.76	6.997
1985	162.26	6.84	11.099
1986	223.76	7.20	16.111
1987	307.33	7.20	22.128
1988	380.15	8.64	32.845
1989	514.69	11.34	58.366
1990	703.42	8.64	60.775
1991	924.16	7.56	69.866
1992	1,175.80	7.56	88.890
1993	1,520.35	10.98	166.934
1994	2,151.88	10.98	236.276
1995	2,966.23	10.98	325.692
1996	3,852.08	8.33	320.878

Data source and note: (1) This table is calculated based on Table B here, Table 4.2 of Yi Gang (1996a) and Table 3.9 of *China Financial Outlook* (1997). (2) *S* in this table refers to the urban and rural household deposit amount.

Table G BD: 1979–1996

	BC (billion Yuan)	I_I/BC (%)	BD (billion Yuan)
1979	216.3	1.3	2.812
1980	262.4	3.0	7.872
1981	304.8	0.6	1.829
1982	341.5	1.3	4.440
1983	388.5	0.5	1.943
1984	508.0	0.04	0.203
1985	643.1	0.2	1.286
1986	820.6	1.1	9.027
1987			85.0
1988			111.0
1989			156.0
1990			174.0
1991			186.2
1992			300.0
1993			650.0

(*Continued*)

Table G (Continued)

	BC (billion Yuan)	I_l/BC (%)	BD (billion Yuan)
1994			700.0
1995			800.0
1996			1,000.0

Data source and note: (1) I_l/BC in this table refers to the proportion of the enterprise deficits covered by banks in *BC*, calculated based on relevant data in *China Statistical yearbook* (1992) and *China Financial Yearbook* (1992). The values of *BD* here are smaller than practical conditions. Because state-owned banks started releasing the loans for fixed assets after 1980 and the state replaced appropriations to state-owned enterprises with loans in 1985, many enterprises were established without any capital or with less capital but mainly relying on loans. From 1984 to 1988, the circulating fund appropriated by the treasury amounted to 36.5 billion Yuan, and, from 1985 to 1988, the enterprise loss covered by the state amounted to 149.37 billion Yuan (Cai Zhongzhi, 1992, pages 245–224). Under these circumstances, a part of loans would definitely transfer to be bad debts regardless of the efficiency in fund use. (2) The values of BD between 1987 and 1990 are the financing amount provided by the state to deficits of state-owned enterprises introduced from Table A3.1 of the World Bank (1996b), which are quite close to bad debts of state-owned banks. (3) There are many opinions in the theoretical realm on *BD* values between 1991 and 1996. This table does the best to make estimates based on some authoritative documents, which are not listed here since too many documents are involved.

Table H The ratio of benefit and cost of financial control by the state: 1979–1996

	(%)						
	SE	BT	FS	MC	SC	SI	BD
1979	30.38	3.42	66.19	9.92		25.55	64.54
1980	22.77	0.58	76.64	4.97		20.44	74.59
1981	18.69	0.83	80.48	14.06		52.19	33.75
1982	14.81	8.33	76.86	10.96		41.58	47.46
1983	26.87	7.70	65.42	14.13		62.32	23.55
1984	40.21	18.17	41.63	19.80		77.93	2.26
1985	65.55	15.44	19.01	13.27	7.34	71.14	8.24
1986	36.09	24.51	39.40	11.90	6.26	52.45	29.39
1987	17.80	21.72	60.47	4.48	2.13	19.29	74.10
1988	32.96	15.27	51.77	4.55	2.47	21.23	71.76
1989	30.60	8.31	61.10	3.38	1.97	25.77	68.88
1990	37.42	11.04	51.54	3.27	2.09	24.50	70.14
1991	38.54	8.19	53.27	3.63	2.42	25.63	68.32
1992	34.82	6.65	58.52	3.22	2.15	21.63	73.00
1993	39.70	5.82	54.48	1.98	1.55	19.71	76.76
1994	50.00	2.43	47.57	3.25	2.36	23.82	70.57
1995	37.21	5.35	57.44	3.48	2.36	27.24	66.91
1996	58.26	3.52	38.21	3.61	2.67	22.77	70.95
Mean	35.15	9.29	55.55	7.44	2.98	35.29	55.29

Data source: Tables A–G in this appendix.

Bibliography

Aristotle, *Politics*, Beijing: The Commercial Press, 1965.

Bellah, Robert, *Tokugawa Religion: Cultural Origins of Modern Japan*, Beijing: Joint Publishing, 1997.

Bodde, Derk, *Fundamentals of Law in China*, refer to Derk Bodde, *Law in Imperial China*, Nanjing: Jiangsu People's Publishing House, 1995, Page 1–35.

Bodde, Derk, *State Qin and Empire Qin*, refer to Denis Twitchett and Michael Loewe, *The Cambridge History of China of Qin and Han*, Beijing: China Social Science Press, 1992, Page 34–116.

Braudel, Fernand, *Material Civilization, Economics and Capitalism 15th–18th Centuries*, Beijing: Joint Publishing, 1993.

Buchanan, James, *Liberty, Market and State*, Shanghai: Shanghai Joint Publishing Press, 1988.

Cai Zhongzhi, *Study on Formation of Inflation in China*, Beijing: China Renmin University Press, 1992.

Chen Jianbo, Property Right Structure of Rural Enterprises and Its Influence on Efficiency of Resources Allocation, *Economic Research*, 1995 (9), Page 24–32.

Chen Lai, Traditions of East Asia in Eyes of Modernization Theories, *Reading*, 1997 (3), Page 3–12.

China Financial Yearbook, 1982–1997.

China Statistical Yearbook, Beijing: China Statistics Press, 1982–1997.

China Statisticians Office, *Report on National Realities of China: 1978–1995*, Beijing: China Statistics Press, 1996.

Cui Zhiyuan, *Thoughts on Development of the Shareholding System and Stock Market in China*, refer to China (Hainan) Institute for Reform and Development, *Theories and Reality of Transition to a Market Economy*, Beijing: Xinhua Publishing House, 1995, Page 202–206.

De Wulf, Luc & Goldsbrough, David, *The Evolving Role of Monetary Policy in China*, IMF Staff Papers, June 1986, Page 209–242.

Eggertsson, Thrainn, *Principles of Neoinstitutional Economics*, Beijing: The Commercial Press, 1990, Page 76–83.

Fan Gang, *Dual-Track Transition: Achievements and Issues of Gradual Marketization in China*, refer to Fan Gang, *Lead to the Market (1978–1993)*, Shanghai: Shanghai People's Publishing House, 1994.

Fan Gang, *My Understandings of Several Issues of Economics Methodology*, refer to Jiangsu People's Publishing House, *Confession of 100 Economists of Modern China* (1), Nanjing: Jiangsu People's Publishing House, 1992, Page 881–903.

Fan Gang, *Political Economic Analysis of the Gradual Reform*, Shanghai: Shanghai Far East Publishing House, 1996.

Fan Gang et al., *Outline of Macro-Economic Theories of Public Ownership*, Shanghai: Shanghai Joint Publishing Press, 1990.

Fan Yifei, *Analysis of the Process and Distribution Pattern of National Income*, Beijing: China Renmin University Press, 1994.

Fairbank, John King & Reischauer, Edwin, *China: Traditions and Reform*, Nanjing: Jiangsu People's Publishing House, 1995, Page 58–77.

Fei Xiaotong, *From the Soil: The Foundations of Chinese Society*, Beijing: Joint Publishing, 1985.

Fry, M. J., Models of Financially Repressed Developing Economics, *World Development*, September 1982 10(9).

Fry, M. J., Money and Capital of Financial Deepening in Economic Development?, *Journal of Money, Credit and Banking*, November 1978 10(4).

Fry, M. J., *Money, Interest and Banking in Economic Development*, Baltimore: The Johns Hopkins University Press, 1988.

Gao Peiyong, *Research on the Operating Mechanism of National Debts*, Beijing: The Commercial Press, 1995.

Gelb, A. H., *Financial Policies, Growth and Efficiency*, World Bank Working Paper, Country Economics Department, 1989, No. WPS 202.

Gernet, Jacques, *China Social History*, translated by Geng Sheng, Nanjing: Jiangsu People's Publishing House, 1995, Page 55–70.

Goldsmith, Raymond W., *Financial Structure and Development*, Shanghai: Shanghai Joint Publishing Press, 1988.

Guo Kesha, *China: Economic Growth and Structural Changes during the Reform*, Shanghai: Shanghai Joint Publishing Press, 1993.

He Huaihong, *Hereditary Society and Its Disintegration: The Spring and Autumn Period in the History of China*, Beijing: Joint Publishing, 1996.

Hellmann, Thomas, Murdock, Kevin & Stiglitz, Joseph, *Financial Restraint: A New Analysis Framework*, refer to Aoki Masahiko, KimHyung-Ki and Masahiro Okuno, *The Role of Government in Economic Development in East Asia*, London: Oxford University Press, Beijing: China Economic Publishing House, 1998.

Hicks, John, *A Theory of Economic History*, Beijing: The Commercial Press, 1987.

Hogheinz, Roy & Calder, Kent, *The Eastasia Edge*, Nanjing: Jiangsu People's Publishing House, 1982, Page 53–64.

Hong Yinxing et al., *Theory of Development Capital*, Beijing: People's Publishing House, 1992.

Huang Xiaoxiang, Inflation and Economic Growth, *Management World*, 1988 (2), Page 47–56.

Huntington, Samuel, *Political Order in Changing Societies*, Beijing: Joint Publishing, 1989, Page 152–160.

Hu Ruyin, *Low Efficiency Economics: Rethinking of Theory of the Centralized System*, Shanghai: Shanghai Joint Publishing Press, 1992.

International Monetary Fund (IMF), *International Financial Statistics*, Author: Washington, D.C., 1983.

International Monetary Fund, *New Stage of Economic Reform in China*, Beijing: China Financial Publishing House, 1995.

Kato Shigeshi, *Chinese Economic History (1–4)*, Beijing: The Commercial Press, 1959–1963.

Kennedy, Paul, *The Rise and Fall of the Great Powers*, Beijing: China Economic Publishing House, 1989, Page 4–10.

Ke Rongzhu, The Equilibrium Issue of Long-Term Negotiation: Institutional Evolution and Game–Concurrently on Improvement of the Coase Theorem, *Chinese Social Sciences Quarterly (Hong Kong)*, 1997, Spring and Summer Volume, Page 78–93.

Kitchen, R. L., *Finance for the Developing Countries*, Hoboken, NJ: John Wiley & Sons, 1986.

Lewis, W. Arthur, *The Theory of Economic Growth*, Shanghai: Shanghai Joint Publishing Press, Shanghai People's Publishing House, 1994.

Li Daokui, Theory of Ambiguous Property Rights in the Transitional Economy, *Economic Research*, 1995 (4), Page 42–50.

Li Yue et al., *The Structure of the Industrial Sector of China*, Beijing: China Renmin University Press, 1983.

Liang Shuming, *Theory of Rural Construction*, refer to *Collected Works of Liang Shuming*, Volume 2, Jinan: Shandong People's Publishing House, 1990.

Lin Yifu, *Economics Theory of Institutional Evolution: Induced Changes and Compulsory Changes*, refer to Ronald Coase, Arman Alchian and Douglass North, *Property Rights and Institutional Evolution: Collected Works of Translations of the Property Rights School and Neoinstitutional School*, Shanghai: Shanghai Joint Publishing Press, Shanghai People's Publishing House, 2004, Page 371–409.

Lin Yifu et al., *The Chinese Miracle: Development Strategy and Economic Reform*, Shanghai: Shanghai Joint Publishing Press, Shanghai People's Publishing House, 1994.

Lin Yifu et al., *Complete Information and Reform of State-Owned Enterprises*, Shanghai: Shanghai Joint Publishing Press, Shanghai People's Publishing House, 1997.

Lin Yifu et al., *Needham Puzzle: Why the Industrial Revolution Were Not Originated from China*, refer to *Institutions, Technologies and Agricultural Development of China*, Shanghai: Shanghai Joint Publishing Press, Shanghai People's Publishing House, 1992.

Lu Liling & Shen Ying, *Debt Settlement in Reorganization of State-Owned Enterprises*, Beijing: Economic Science Publishing House, 1997.

Maddison, Angus, *Monitoring the World Economy: 1820–1992*, Beijing: Reform Publishing House, 1997, Page 27–29.

Ma Hong, *Encyclopedia of Modern Chinese Economy*, Beijing: China Social Science Press, 1982.

Mckinnon, Ronald I., *Money and Capital in Economic Development*, Shanghai: Shanghai Joint Publishing Press, 1988.

Mckinnon, Ronald I., *The Sequence of Economic Marketization: Financial Control during the Transition to Market Economy*, Shanghai: Shanghai Joint Publishing Press, Shanghai People's Publishing House, 1996.

Michio Morishima, *Why Japan "Succeeds"*, Chengdu: Sichuan People's Publishing House, 1986.

Murphy, K., Shleifer, A. & Vishny, R., The Transition to A Market Economy: Pitfalls of Partial Reforms, *The Quarterly Journal of Economics*, August 1992.

Naughton, B., Reforming Planned Economy: Is China Unique? in Lee, C., and Reisen, H., eds, *From Reform to Growth: China and Other Countries in Transition*, Paris: Development Center, OECD, 1994.

Nee, V., Organizational Dynamics of Market Transition: Hybrid Forms, Property Rights, and Mixed Economy in China, *Administrative Science Quarterly*, 1992 37(1).

North, Douglass, *Institutions, Institutional Changes and Economic Performance*, Shanghai: Shanghai Joint Publishing Press, 1990.

North, Douglass, *Structure and Change in Economic History*, London: W. W. Norton & Company, 1981.

Paleri, Henry, *Neoliberalism Economics of America*, Beijing: Peking University Press, 1985.

Panel of China Reform and Development Report, *1978–1994 China Reform and Development Report: The Path of China*, Beijing: China Financial & Economic Publishing House, 1995.

Panel of China Reform and Development Report, *1992–1993 China Reform and Development Report: New Breakthroughs and New Challenges*, Beijing: China Financial & Economic Publishing House, 1994.

People's Bank of China, *1979–1986 China Monetary Flow Investigation*, Beijing: China Finance Publishing House, 1988.

People's Bank of China, *China Financial Outlook (1994–1997)*.

Powelson, J. *Property Ownerships in Development of China: Historical Comparison*, refer to Wang Xi and J. Dorn, *Chinese Economic Reform: Issues and Prospects*, Shanghai: Fudan University Press, 1994, Page 118–132.

Qian Yingyi, *Corporate Management Structure Reform and Financing Reform of China*, refer to Aoki Masahiko and Qian Yingyi, *Corporate Management Structure in the Transitional Economy: Internal Control and the Role of Bank*, Beijing: China Economic Publishing House, 1995, Page 113–150.

Qian Yingyi, *Lessons and Relevance of the Japanese Main Bank System for Financial Reform in China*, Stanford: Stanford University Press, 1993.

Qin Duo, Money Demand and Supply Since the Reform, *Economic Research*, 1997 (10), Page 16–25.

Reischauer, Edwin, *Contemporary Japanese: Tradition and Reform*, Beijing: The Commercial Press, 1992, Page 103–184.

Research Group of the Industrial and Commercial Bank of China Hunan Province Branch, Discussion on Excessive Debts of State-Owned Enterprises, *China Industrial Economy*, 1996 (4), Page 26–34.

Roland, Gérard, *Political Economics in Ownership Transformation in Eastern Europe*, refer to Aoki Masahiko and Qian Yingyi, *Corporate Management Structure in the Transitional Economy: Internal Control and the Role of Bank*, Beijing: China Economic Publishing House, 1995, Page 43–72.

Sachs, J. & Woo, W., Structural Factors in the Economic Reforms of China, Eastern Europe, and the Former Soviet Union, *Economic Policy*, April 1994a, 9 (18), Page 101–145.

Sachs, J. & Woo, W., Understanding the Reform Experiences of China, Eastern Europe and Russia, in C. Lee and H. Reisen, eds, *From Reform to Growth: China and Other Countries in Transition*, Paris: Development Center, OECD, 1994b.

Schultz, Theodore W., *Constant Improvements of Economic Value of Institutions and People*, refer to *Property Rights and Institutional Evolution: Collected Works of Translations of the Property Rights School and Neoinstitutional School*, Shanghai: Shanghai Joint Publishing Press, Shanghai People's Publishing House, 1995.

Shapiro, Edward, *Macroeconomic Analysis*, Beijing: China Social Science Press, 1985.

Shen Ying, International Comparison of the Modes for Reorganization of Banks and Enterprises, *China Securities Daily*, 1997–07–03, 1997–07–10, 1997–07–31.

Sheng Hong, *Labor Division and Transaction: Analysis of the Application of a General Theory to Unprofessional Issues of China*, Shanghai: Shanghai Joint Publishing Press, Shanghai People's Publishing House, 1994.

Sheng Hong, Research on the Transition of Marketization in China, *Economic Research,* 1996 (1), Page 68–80.

Shi Jinchuan et al., Emerging Non-Government Financial Sector during Market Deepening– with Zhejiang Road & Bridge Urban Cooperative as an Instance, *Economic Research,* 1997 (12), Page 45–50.

State Administration for Foreign Exchange, *Report on Development of Foreign Debts of China 1995,* Beijing: China Financial & Economic Publishing House, 1995.

Stiglitz, J. E., *Economics,* New York: W. W. Norton, 1993.

Stiglitz, Joseph, The Role of Government in Economic Development, *Economic Herald,* 1997, Page 1–8.

Stiglitz, J. E. & Weiss, A., Credit Rationing in Markets with Imperfect Information, *American Economics Review,* 1981 (71), Page 393–410.

Suzuki Shuo, *Financial Theory of Modern China,* Shanghai: Shanghai Joint Publishing Press, 1991, Page 85–123.

Tian Guoqiang, Endogenous Property Ownership Theory and Stable Transition of the Economic System, *Economic Research,* 1996 (11), Page 11–20.

Tigar, Michael & Levy, Madeleine, *Rise of Law and Capitalism,* Shanghai: Academia Press, 1996, Page 3–53.

Wang Jizu, Theory of Financial Deepening: Development and Influence in Two Decades, *Nankai Economic Studies,* 1997 (5), Page 34–44.

Wang Jun, Total Quantity of Capital Outflow of China and Structure Analysis, *Reform,* 1996 (5), Page 91–101.

Wang Shaoguang & Hu Angang, *Research Report on State Capacity of China,* refer to *Centralization and Decentralization: The Relationship between Central and Local Governments,* Beijing: Economic Science Publishing House, 1996, Page 12–42.

Weber, Max, *Confucianism and Taoism,* translated by Hong Tianfu, Nanjing: Jiangsu People's Publishing House, 1995.

The World Bank, *1989 World Development Report: Financial System and Development,* Beijing: China Financial & Economic Publishing House, 1989.

The World Bank, *1996 World Development Report: From Plan to Market,* Beijing: China Financial & Economic Publishing House, 1996a.

The World Bank, *China in 2020: Development Challenges in the New Century,* Beijing: China Financial & Economic Publishing House, 1997.

The World Bank, *China: Macro-Economic Stability and Industrial Growth,* Beijing: China Financial & Economic Publishing House, 1990.

The World Bank, *Chinese Economy: Inflation Management and Reform Deepening,* Beijing: China Financial & Economic Publishing House, 1996b.

Wu Jiesi, *Study on Behaviors of State-Owned Commercial Banks of China,* Beijing: China Financial Publishing House, 1996.

Wu Jinglian et al., *Strategic Reorganization of the State-Owned Economy,* Beijing: China Development Publishing House, 1998.

Wu Shaoxin, Financial Risks of China: Situation, Cause and Prevention, *Financial System Reform,* 1997 (8), Page 2–15.

Wu Xiaoling et al., China State-Owned Enterprises–Reorganization of Bank Debts, *Comparative Economic and Social Systems,* 1995 (3), Page 11–21.

Wu Xiaoling et al., Tracking Study on the Financial System Reform in China, *Reform,* 1997 (3), Page 64–75, 1997 (4), Page 83–98.

Xiao Geng, Financial Reform of China: Institutional Evolution, Theories and Policies, *Chinese Social Sciences Quarterly (Hong Kong),* 1995, Autumn Volume, Page 52–65.

Xiao Geng, *Property Rights and Economic Reform of China*, Beijing: China Social Science Press, 1997.

Xie Ping, *Selections of the Financial System of China*, Shanghai: Shanghai Far East Publishing House, 1996.

Xie Ping & Yu Qiao, Control over Monetary Aggregate during Economic Marketization of China, *Management World*, 1996 (4), Page 45–55, 1996 (5), Page 29–40.

Xu Jian, *Monetary Control during Economic Transition of China*, Beijing: China Financial & Economic Publishing House, 1997.

Xu Xiaonian, Information, Enterprise Monitoring and Fluidity, *Reform*, 1996 (4), Page 77–86, 1996 (5), Page 39–43.

Xu Zhuoyun, *The Ancient*, Taipei: Linking Publishing, 1982.

Xu Zhuoyun, *History of Western Zhou*, Beijing: Joint Publishing, 1994.

Xue Muqiao, *Research on Socialist Economic Issues of China*, Beijing: People's Publishing House, 1979.

Yang Ruilong, *The Property Right System of Modern Enterprises*, Beijing: China Renmin University Press, 1996.

Yang Ruilong, Three Stages for Institutional Evolution of China–Concurrently on Institutional Innovations of Local Governments, *Economic Research*, 1998 (1), Page 3–10.

Yang Xiaokai, *Contemporary Economics and Chinese Economy*, Beijing: China Social Science Press, 1997.

Yang Xiaowei, Selection of Methods of Chinese Economics and Others–Concurrently on Comments on Casebook, *Chinese Social Sciences Quarterly (Hong Kong)*, 1997, Spring and Summer Volume, Page 254–258.

Yi Gang, Analysis of the Financial Assets Structure of China and Policy Connotation, *Economic Research*, 1996b (12), Page 26–33.

Yi Gang, *Money, Banks and Financial Market of China: 1984–1993*, Shanghai: Shanghai Joint Publishing Press, Shanghai People's Publishing House, 1996a.

Yi Gang, Money Demand and Inflation of China, *Economic Research*, 1995 (5), Page 51–58.

Zang Xuheng, *Analysis of the Consumption Function of China*, Shanghai: Shanghai Joint Publishing Press, Shanghai People's Publishing House, 1995.

Zhang Chunlin, Discussion on Reform of State-Owned Enterprises from the Perspective of Bankruptcy and Merger Pilot, *Reform*, 1997 (4), Page 9–18.

Zhang Chunlin, On Debts of State-Owned Enterprises, *Reform*, 1996 (1), Page 22–23.

Zhang Fengbo, *Macroeconomic Structure and Policies of China*, Beijing: China Financial & Economic Publishing House, 1988.

Zhang Jie, *Analysis of State-Owned Financial Institutional Changes of China*, Beijing: Economic Science Publishing House, 1998.

Zhang Jie, Bad Debts and Settlement of State-Owned Banks, *Economists*, 1997b (6), Page 55–63.

Zhang Jie, *Economic Analysis of Financial Growth of China*, Beijing: China Economic Publishing House, 1995b.

Zhang Jie, Intervention by Local Governments and Variation of the Financial System, *Economic Research*, 1996 (3), Page 21–26.

Zhang Jie, Monetization Process, Financial Control and Reform Dilemma of China, *Economic Research*, 1997a (8), Page 20–25.

Zhang Jie, Property Rights in the Economic System Reform of China, *Economists*, 1994 (4), Page 5–6.

Zhang Jie, *Puzzle of Round Heaven and Square Earth: Investigation on Monetary History and Culture of China*, Beijing: China Finance Publishing House, 1993.

Zhang Jie, Review on Financial Reform of China and Approach for Further Reform, *Economic Research*, 1995a (5), Page 3–10.

Zhang Jun, *Dual-Track Economics: Economic Reform of China (1978–1992)*, Shanghai: Shanghai Joint Publishing Press, Shanghai People's Publishing House, 1997a.

Zhang Jun, Informal Financial Sector in Rural Area of China after Reform: Wenzhou Case, *Chinese Social Sciences Quarterly (Hong Kong)*, 1997b, Autumn Volume, Page 22–37.

Zhang Jun, *Modern Property Rights Economics*, Shanghai: Shanghai Joint Publishing Press, Shanghai People's Publishing House, 1994.

Zhang Shuguang, Promote Demonstration and Integrate into the Mainstream–Acknowledgement to Dr. Zhou Qiren and Zhang Jun, *Chinese Social Sciences Quarterly (Hong Kong)*, 1997, Spring and Summer Volume, Page 247–253.

Zhang Shuguang, *Relaxing the Control on Grain Price and Cancelling Grain Coupons: Research on Changes of the Grains Procurement and Sale System of China*, refer to *Case Study on Institutional Changes of China*, (Volume 1), Shanghai: Shanghai People's Publishing House, 1995b, Page 266–303.

Zhang Shuguang, State Capacity and Institutional Reform and Social Transformation–Concurrently on China State Capacity Report, *China Review (Hong Kong)*, 1995a (3).

Zhang Weiying, *Game Theory and Information Economics*, Shanghai: Shanghai Joint Publishing Press, Shanghai People's Publishing House, 1996.

Zhang Weiying, Rational Thinking on Reform of State-Owned Enterprises of China, *China Business Times*, 1995–01–23.

Zhang Yichun & Zhou Yinggang, Asymmetric Information, Enterprise Reform and Securities Market, *Economic Research*, 1997 (5), Page 24–30.

Zheng Xianbing, *Introduction to the Interest Rate*, Beijing: China Finance Publishing House, 1991.

Zheng Yefu, *Cost Theory: A New Perspective of Sociology*, Beijing: Joint Publishing, 1995, Page 41–56.

Zhou Qiren, *Changes of the Relation between the State and Land Ownership: A Review on Economic Institutional Changes*, refer to Beijing Tianze Economic Research Institute, *Economics of China: 1994*, Shanghai: Shanghai People's Publishing House, 1995, Page 26–89.

Zhou Xiaochuan, Re-Establishment of the Relation between Enterprises and Banks, *Reform*, 1994 (6), Page 72–83.

Zhou Xiaochuan et al., *Enterprise Reform: Mode Selection and Supporting Design*, Beijing: China Economic Publishing House, 1994.

Zhu Ling, Thinking on Re-Organization and Extension of Rural Financial Organizations, *Reform*, 1995 (4), Page 12–14.

Zuo Dapei, Exploration on Modernized Economics of China–Comment on Economics of China 1994, *Economic Research*, 1996 (4), Page 61–63.

Index